FOLLOW

YOUR

CALLING

Find & Follow the Path God
Has Created for You

John Bradley
and
Nelson Malwitz

Online Supplemental Resources

1. Finding Organizations That Share Your Passion
Some of the exercises in this book will help you translate your passion into specific names of ministry organizations. To help you, we recommend the use of the Ministry Web Directory at *ministrywebdirectory.org*—a national listing of ministry organizations provided by Christian colleges and seminaries. On the website, begin with the instructions on how to complete a *ministry search*, which provides you with a *primary search report*. This report will give you names of ministry organizations sorted by the state and city of your choice, and includes valid contact information. If the database does not provide results for your city, broaden your search to your state or to the USA. The service is free; all you have to do is register. You can also search for ministry job vacancies and student internship postings.

2. Finding Mission Organizations
You can match your passion and your skills to global mission organizations through the Finisher Project website. After completing a questionnaire, your qualifications are matched to mission organizations who have listed needs for those qualities. This service is useful to people of all ages, but was originally developed for those of retirement age looking to serve in cross-cultural settings. Most listed opportunities require raising your own support. The service is free. Go to *finishers.org*.

3. Discovering Your Talent Strengths
Some of the exercises in this book will help you identify your God-given *Communicational*, *Relational* and *Functional* (task-oriented) talent strengths. You'll use these strengths to identify your ideal ministry job duties. For most, these exercises are sufficient to get a good picture of your strengths. However, if you want a more objective, more detailed evaluation of your talents, you can go online and preview both the Talent Discovery Guide and the Career Match. Each provides higher levels of aptitude testing and assessment. You can look at free samples at *IDAKgroup.com*. There are additional costs to use these assessment tools.

Acknowledgements

We would like to thank the following individuals, who have helped make this book a published reality.

To Brian Smith, our editor, we offer our first and foremost thanks. You have stayed true and helped us so many times overcome hurdles, smooth out tangles, meet deadlines and most importantly keep the process going over the last two years. You are truly a professional. Keep up the good work.

We also thank Karen Pickering, who helped us with Dawson Media's initial publishing steps. Also thanks to Athena McDaniels at Dawson Media for finishing up the work and covering all of the details. Our thanks also to Rachel Eck, our cover artist, who was able to take vague concepts and make them a visual reality.

Special thanks to Judy Drais and Cindy Ludeman, who assisted in typing portions of the text and proofreading. We also acknowledge our wives, Marge Malwitz and Cathy Bradley, for their support, as well as the staff at Finishers Project and the IDAK Group. All of you have been such a great team; we are blessed to have your help.

Contents

Foreword
by Lloyd Reeb

Over the past decade I have coached thousands of people in midlife transition, helping them get clear about their strengths and passions and mission, get free of what's holding them back and get going on the adventure of a lifetime. The thrill for me is watching others find their love and overflow with delight.

When I was in the confusion of finding my calling for the second half of my life, my mentor Bob Buford said to me, "If you focus on your strengths, your weaknesses will become irrelevant." Over the past fifteen plus years I have partnered with Nelson Malwitz in ministry. I have seen this truth not only in his life but in mine as well. Both of us are making the most of the Lord's wiring in us to make a difference.

In Luke 12, Jesus warned us about greed, and He told us that to live a good life is to live like a house servant who knows their assignment and lives it out. He went on to say that to us who have been given much, much will be demanded. This book provides a biblical basis for the how and why of giving back to the Lord what He as given to you.

Lloyd Reeb is primary spokesperson for HalfTime and author of *From Success to Significance* and *The Second Half: Real Stories, Real Adventures, Real Significance.*

Testimonial
by Jay Carty

After I finished playing ball with the Lakers, I was a job hopper. I never got fired; I just couldn't find a good fit. I'd last about a year and a half and then I'd be off to something else. After years of frustration, I thought getting into the ministry in some way would solve my restlessness. But helping people isn't enough if you're not in the right slot.

Through my wife, Mary, I was introduced to John Bradley and discovered my natural talents. John helped me tailor a job description around my strengths. I spent the next twenty-five-plus years doing what I loved and loving what I did. Instead of dreading each day, I would wake up invigorated and eager to start. That was my world after I allowed my God-given wiring to shape my direction.

During my travels as an iterant preacher and church growth consultant I would often encounter pastors who were clearly in the wrong slots. They knew something was wrong but didn't know what else to do. I've referred close to a hundred people to John, to discover their natural talents and their best-fit role. John and his team are batting 100 percent with my referrals, so I'd like to refer you to this process. Granted, a book approach is less involved than meeting with a counselor, but for most individuals, just learning the truth about one's inner design can be a freeing experience.

This practical, proven approach, which has helped thousands, will help you discover your God-given wiring. You really can do what you love and love what you do.

Jay Carty is the author of twelve books, including the bestselling *Coach Wooden One-On-One* and Medallion of Excellence Award-winning *Coach Wooden's Pyramid of Success*. Jay and his wife, Mary, make their home in Maui and have two grown children.

Introduction
From Stressed Out to Satisfying Service

I'm forty-five and I still don't know what I want to be when I grow up."

Greg obviously expected that his declaration would elicit from me a gasp or an empathetic "oh, my." He was an electrical engineer working for a Fortune 500 company, outwardly successful by most people's standards. Stable family, stable job and very good income.

But I (John) had been doing my job too long to be surprised. I am the founder and president of IDAK Group, a business that serves both marketplace and ministry leaders in finding what they do best. And Greg's statement was one I'd heard, with minor variations, hundreds of times. I smiled to convey understanding and acceptance, then explained to Greg that he was part of a large segment of the workforce who, at midlife, struggle with their identity—outwardly successful, inwardly wrestling mightily with disappointment and dissatisfaction.

"But," I said, "you are one of the brave few who are willing to get off the treadmill and ask, 'For what purpose am I giving my life? Is it just so that a corporation can make a profit? Or might I devote the remainder of my life to something greater, something lasting?'"

I leaned forward. "Thank you," I said, "for being honest and brave enough to consider your future. I believe each of us hopes that our life will count for something. You have taken a bold step forward, assessing whether your current direction is taking you toward that goal." And so we began the process of evaluating Greg's passion—passion to make a difference that would serve God, his Creator—and discovering how God had wired him.

Maybe you're at midlife, like Greg. Or younger. Or older. Nelson and I have met with thousands of individuals of all ages and found that each believer in Christ has an inner voice asking, "Why am I here?" Yearning to do something meaningful, something that counts for the King. Maybe a part-time or volunteer role. Maybe full-time. Perhaps for a season, as a timeout. Or for the second half of life. Or for a lifetime.

Each of us hopes that our life will count for something.

Whatever the circumstances, the first two steps toward God's answers for you are the same. First, you need to listen to your passion—that inner voice—and translate its message into a tangible life direction. And second, you need to evaluate your gifting and discern the doors of life opportunity it opens for you.

Through this book—and through additional online resources we provide for in-depth support—we are offering our combined sixty years of experience helping men and women find their calling. As you process the ideas and exercises in this book, we will help empower you to do the same, leading you step by step, until you're contacting real people who are, today, doing your ideal ministry job. We'll help you connect with like-minded, like-hearted organizations where you can plunge with joy into the next chapter of your life—maybe the most exciting chapter yet!

> For I know the thoughts that I think toward you, says the LORD, thoughts of peace and not of evil, to give you a future and a hope.
>
> —Jeremiah 29:11

With your hope-filled future in view, we urge you to strike out on your journey of self-discovery. But maybe you're saying, "I've been down this road before." You may have made several attempts to start a new life chapter, to reinvent yourself. We have met many people who have taken early retirement—or otherwise departed from their previous career—and embarked on short-term mission trips or volunteered in a local ministry, hoping to discover that special niche for service. Many end up disappointed with the hit-and-miss approach. We're offering a different path, one that's been carefully mapped out by many who have gone before you. Take courage. We believe this journey will lead to an outcome you'll appreciate.

Faith for a Great Finish

Hi, I'm Nelson. Some recognition has come my way in the founding of the Finishers Project—a ministry that provides information, challenge and pathways for people to enter missions from any point in their careers. My efforts have focused on opening doors for people to use their considerable talents in ministry, short-term and long-term, home and abroad.

One of the steps for launching the Finishers Project was an extensive research project in 1998, in which we interviewed six hundred evangelical baby boomers in missions-minded churches regarding their next stage of life. Among many other questions, we asked about the possibility of their serving in missions and the barriers they perceived in the way. We learned that neither quality of life nor even family considerations stood as the biggest barriers between these people and missions. Instead, their greatest concerns were:

1. *Is this God's will for my life?* and
2. *How will the finances work?*

God's call on our lives is to be actively moving forward.

This book deals with issue number one. And often if that is fully settled, issue number two becomes less of a barrier to overcome.

God's call on our lives is to be actively moving forward along His path. That is probably why you picked up this book—seeking to know God's will for your next steps. Actually, the answer that comes back from Scripture is clear: The Lord calls us to ask for wisdom—wisdom defined biblically as "skillful living"; and wisdom means, in part, to follow the gifting He has given us. This sounds practically simple, but it can be emotionally difficult. God calls us to give back (more accurately, to *live* back) to Him what He has given to us—our experience and our expertise, our talents and our training, our very lives—for maximum impact and maximum joy.

That path is different for everyone. We offer this book as a way of discovering God's path, which has been uniquely set out for you. If you authentically seek Him first, you won't go wrong. Will you seek Him (first, above all else) and His direction—the life direction that will bring you greatest fulfillment? Will you trust the Lord to do a better job guiding your life than you can by yourself? Are you willing to take a risk for God, taking Him at His word to uphold His end of the bargain?

For some, the first risk is simply getting into the game. In Revelation 6 we learn to our surprise that saints who have preceded us in death are monitoring events on earth. They have done their part, and now they are filling the stands and we are the ones on the playing field. Maybe for you, the first step toward following your calling is a mental shift into willingness to take action. It's your time!

God calls us to live back to Him what He has given to us.

And don't wait for God to pronounce His personalized plan for you in bold, scripted skywriting. He may use dramatic methods for some of His people (like the apostle Paul on the road to Damascus in Acts 9), but His more typical method is to direct *your* efforts in seeking to understand your personal passions and the special abilities with which He has equipped you for His work.

Will you trust Him to guide that self-examination process, even if it takes some time? His plans for you include even your next steps of self-discovery. He won't let you down.

A Lifelong Journey

Both of us share a passion to encourage and challenge today's adult generations to become intentionally, fully engaged in making a difference. This book is a product of our shared passion, and we want you to know, without any doubt: *You can make a difference in God's world.* The best way for you to discover your place is to take the gifts and talents He's given you and give them back to Him—by exercising them in your first or second career, in part-time or volunteer ministry, in the years ahead.

In fact, we've discovered that, once a person begins operating in his or her God-given strengths, he or she typically engages so fully in serving the Lord and others that words like "sacrifice" and "obstacle" do not apply—they're replaced with themes like "fulfillment" and "opportunity" and "joy."

There is always more to learn, another stage to the adventure.

We deliberated carefully over the title of this book. We could have called it *Finding Your Calling*. But we were concerned this might suggest that one's calling is static, that once you find it your pursuit is over. That is not the case. For many people, God's calling changes with new life seasons and leads to ever greater conquests as we gain maturity.

We might have titled this book *Fulfilling Your Calling*. But, again, we will never arrive this side of eternity. There is always more to learn, another stage to the adventure. Even Jesus didn't say "It is finished" until the last moment of His natural earthly life.

The title we chose is *Follow Your Calling*, suggesting a continuous journey. This journey involves, on the one hand, our remaining daily in eye contact with the Lord, depending on His prompting for the next stage or the next step. On the other hand, He also calls us to take active initiative. The journey is one of lifelong cooperation between our efforts and God's sovereign empowerment.

Obligation or Adoration?

Before we launch into this journey, let's take a moment for heart preparation. One thing that I (John) have learned in life is that *why* I do something is often as important as *what* I do. One's inward motive can make all the difference between being a world-changer and being ineffective, even if one's outward actions are the same in both cases.

In my adult life I've striven to do the very utmost for God with what He's given me. But for many years I carried a burden of legalistic guilt that I didn't know how to shake. I would measure the worthiness of my activities, my spending of time and money—even my choice of friends—based on how these would contribute to advancing God's kingdom on earth. I'm not saying this was entirely wrong. In fact, in His Word, God expresses serious displeasure toward those who live in complacency and denial of God's call. That's why He challenges us to spur each other on toward love and good deeds (see Hebrews 10:24). But I was missing the whole point of service. I was making just as serious an error, in the opposite direction, as the person who avoids serving God. The core of my motivation was to earn merit badges, in hopes that I might by my good deeds come to *deserve* a "well done, good and faithful servant" at the final roll call. I forgot that any reward or commendation from God is an undeserved gift from His gracious hand, bought only by the sacrifice of Jesus, never by anything I can do.

My motives have been reshaped by a much more powerful drive—love.

Since those days my motives have been reshaped by a much more powerful drive—namely, love. I've learned to focus, not primarily on the goodness of my actions, but on the goodness of the God for whom I do them. I now seek to serve others, not in order to check them off of my cosmic to-do list, but out of love for them and for God. This love implies forgiving others for the wrongs they've done me, including the "wrong" of not living up to my standard of zeal for obedience. God's love has made me a more accepting and patient man.

My heart motive was 180-degrees reversed when I met Jesus in this passage:

> Then one of them, a lawyer, asked Him a question, testing Him, and saying, "Teacher, which is the great commandment in the law?"
>
> Jesus said to him, "'You shall love the LORD your God with all your heart, with all your soul, and with all your mind.' This is the first and great commandment. And the second is like it: 'You shall love your neighbor as yourself.' On these two commandments hang all the Law and the Prophets."
>
> —Matthew 22:35–40

(Another instrument God has used to reinforce compassion as my motive for service is Dr. Del Tackett's exceptional DVD series *The Truth Project,* produced by Focus on the Family. In his final session, Dr. Tackett challenges the viewer to consider serving out of an inner yearning to express God's love. I highly recommend this to you.)

Do we owe God? Of course, big time. Our obligation to Him is real. But those who are motivated only by duty are operating under the false assumption that they can pay God back. The way of duty-alone ends in exhaustion, disillusion, anxiety, despair and often burnout. The way of adoration is the way of energy, delight and life. It's the "payment" God asks of us. Selfless love toward God and others is the way of greatest kingdom productivity.

John Piper, who for years has championed the life of delight in God, offers advice in his book *Don't Waste Your Life.* Note what he says is *not* life and love for God:

> Oh, how many lives are wasted by people who believe that the Christian life means simply avoiding badness and providing for the family. So there is no adultery, no stealing, no killing, no embezzlement, no fraud—just lots of hard work during the day, and lots of TV and PG-13 videos in the evening (during quality family time), and lots of fun stuff on the weekend—woven around church (mostly). This is life for millions of people. Wasted life. We were created for more.

And so, fellow pilgrim, as we partner with you to map out the next season of your life, we, Nelson and John, encourage you to look prayerfully inward. Consider how you can bring maximum kingdom impact by projecting His love to others in whatever you do. We believe you'll maximize your compassion and effectiveness, while minimizing your internal stress, when you serve according to your passion and God-given gifting. Learning about these aspects of yourself and exercising them in love is the best way to become a vital embodiment of Jesus' call in Matthew 6:19–21:

The way of adoration is the way of energy, delight and life.

> Do not lay up for yourselves treasures on earth, where moth and rust destroy and where thieves break in and steal;

but lay up for yourselves treasures in heaven, where neither moth nor rust destroys and where thieves do not break in and steal. For where your treasure is, there your heart will be also.

Chapter 1
Celebrate Your Next Chapter

Some people understandably chafe at the notion that one's occupation defines him or her. But doesn't the activity that fills the largest portion of your waking hours provide some clue to your God-given makeup? Your identity? We are indeed justified in believing that one's what-I-do is one of several significant measures of a person.

God's purpose for your life is defined in part by the tasks He has assigned for you to perform, the accomplishments He wants you to achieve (Proverbs 22:29).

And He intends that each of us continue to ask "What's next?" until the only *next* remaining is eternity. We succeed in our life's purpose by keeping our eyes always courageously focused forward. We rise to Jesus' challenge, asking, "What will last beyond me?" We seek to make differences right up to the end, keeping in view the eternal impressions we will leave in the ultimate endgame—heaven.

Yes, we look back with gratitude on the lessons and achievements of the past—the half-full glass of our lives—but we also recognize that the glass is half-empty, waiting to be filled, and we build yet further on the foundation of our past. We keep our minds set on "what I do" and "what I *will* do," resisting the stagnant complacency of the one who deals exclusively in "what I *have* done"—the one who perceives a glass-all-full, no-room-for-more life.

There are always new personal and kingdom goals to pursue. We look back and glean the wisdom we've earned by experience, then we capitalize on it as we move forward into the next season...not with a groan of resentful resignation, but with a *hurray* of eager anticipation. The heart that beats with God's heart yearns to define the end of life as Abraham did, "full of years" (Genesis 25:8)—years packed with kingdom conquests.

This book is designed to assist in defining your next stage. It is, looking to the past and present, an exercise in self-discovery. And looking toward the future, it is a planning guide, best completed in the presence of God. Through it, we will help shed light on your passion for kingdom service and your God-given resources. And we will lead you as you define your direction for the next season of your life.

The Right Team, the Right Task

How will we help you? What can you expect of this journey?

First, we'll focus on your personal *passion*. This is what you strongly feel needs doing. It's a cause, the very mention of which makes your heart beat faster. It's the issue or topic that, more than anything else, rivets your focus. When you start talking about it, you have trouble stopping. When you're in the thick of doing it, you lose track of time. It might be something you're involved with now, or maybe something you've only dreamed about. We'll help you identify at least one of your passions (most people have several), so that you can translate it into a tangible direction for your service.

> *Your personal passion is what you strongly feel needs doing.*

Once your passion is identified, you'll begin the process of finding a *team* of like-minded others who share your convictions about what needs doing. This team will be part of an organization that matches your passion, interests and values. Let's say you're interested in reaching out to Spanish-speaking youth with inadequate education. You might, then, begin to set your sights on joining one of many specific ministries to Central or South America. Or maybe you're interested in helping marginalized children avoid the poverty trap. In that case we'll help you identify local orphanages, child protection advocacy groups, and youth education and other organizations that would welcome your involvement.

These first steps—pinpointing your passion and the beginnings of identifying your ideal team—will be the topics of Chapter 2.

Second, we'll go beyond your passion and help you uncover your *gifting*—the set of God-given talents that, when you exercise them, sustain your excitement and keep you feeling alive. Passion alone is not enough to determine your "sweet spot." And determined willpower alone is not enough to keep you going on a task that doesn't involve the exercise of your God-given talents. You'll find deepest and most lasting satisfaction in a ministry job that makes use of the talents God wired into you.

Your gifting is the set of God-given talents that keep you feeling alive.

In seminary I (John) experienced a great *aha!*—one of life's light bulb moments—when I recognized God's role in gifting His people. I was in an Old Testament survey class, reading Exodus. I came across Exodus 31:1–6 and saw the practical implications of this passage for the first time—hundreds of artisans who were called to build the first dwelling place on earth for God, the tabernacle. In summarizing His instructions, the Lord assured Moses and His people, "In the hearts of all who are skillful I have put skill, that they may make all that I have commanded you" (verse 6, NASB). Can you imagine the thrill of being selected to work on that most holy of places? Your reputation would be forever changed. "I helped build the washstand." "My mom contributed to the woven purple fabric for the inner chamber." "My grandfather shaped the copper curtain hooks." Notice that God claimed to have instilled the skill in each of those who were chosen for the building project. And this colossal task required more than artisans; there were schedules to be planned, work crews to be managed, money to be budgeted, materials to be located and stored. Even singers to be selected.

The Hebrew word for "skill" in verse 6 is *chokmah*. This term represents God-given knowhow. This is also the exact word used throughout Proverbs, commonly translated "wisdom." So, connecting the dots, God must intend some connection between the concepts of skill and wisdom. In fact, a thorough study demonstrates that biblical wisdom is, at its root, God-given knowhow.

Do you recall how Solomon and the other authors of Proverbs exhort us to pursue wisdom? It's one of the most important objects to seek in one's life, more precious than gold, silver and gemstones (Proverbs 2). What better way to begin the pursuit of your calling than to seek wisdom? And at least part of that search for wisdom is the discovery of one's God-given skills, one's gifting.

Wisdom is one of the most important objects to seek.

Given this biblical insight you may ask, "Are my God-given skills different from my occupational skills?" Yes and no. For most who enjoy their work, their day-to-day duties probably call upon a good number of their God-given aptitudes. If one is a successful teacher and enjoys the work, then it's reasonable to assume that teaching is one of that person's God-given skills. But especially for those of us who don't always enjoy our work or who find our jobs stressful, it is important to look beyond the job to find one's God-given skills.

In Chapters 3–5 we will assist you in identifying these natural skills. From this point forward, we're going to use the word *talents* as the primary term for your God-given skills and abilities.

Fulfillingly Ever After...

Finally, in Chapters 6–8 we will arrive at the ultimate goals of your journey. We mentioned earlier that we will use your passion to help identify your ideal *team*. Similarly, in Chapter 6 we'll use your gifting to identify your ideal *task*—the best job title, matched to your gifting, for you to perform as part of the team. So, for example, if you join that ministry in Bolivia, your ideal task might be to repair vehicles or organize outreach events or sit quietly with the elderly and infirm. Or in that orphanage you might be the best finance director they've ever had, or a counselor. The job title and duties all depend on the abilities God has hardwired into you.

In Chapter 7 we will arrive at a merging of your ideal *team* and your ideal *task*, and in Chapter 8 we will use these to help you clarify your practical steps into a specific service role. If you've worked through the exercises up to that point, you will probably have a better understanding of yourself and your God-given makeup than you've ever had before. You also will have eliminated most of the risk of yet another disappointment with a mismatched role. Perhaps for the first time ever, you will select a service role in keeping with what stirs both your heart and your hands. That's the formula for success in following your calling.

In these final chapters you'll go beyond theory. We'll coach you through the process of meeting with someone who has the job you are considering, in order to provide validation of your service goal. No, you won't need to travel to Cairo just yet. But you should talk to someone from a ministry organization that fits your passion, who also has the job you are seeking to perform.

Stages in the Journey

With this book summary in mind, before we launch into the process we've just described, let's put your present situation in the context of life's journey. Let's step back and examine the long and all-too-soon-completed road from beginning to end.

As we enter adulthood, we typically experiment with various life directions, learning about ourselves and our options as we go. Eventually we launch into career, marriage, and family. We dream dreams—many of which resonate with our passions and our God-given makeup—but we often become distracted from them by the mundane details and demands of life. By our thirties many of us have matured to the point that others look to us as leaders.

We dream dreams, but we often become distracted.

Also by our thirties we've made our choices about our level of commitment to Christ. Those who have pursued Him and stayed involved in healthy church relationships will find a spiritual and emotional foothold when they encounter shipwreck, like loss of a job, divorce, loss of a parent, or worse, death of a child or spouse. Even though we are wired to accumulate wealth at this life stage, no amount of money can prepare us for such devastating life events. Only those who have laid a spiritual foundation in Christ—or who finally learn to seek Him—will find the reserves to stay on track through midlife and beyond. Also during these years, if we learn to build on our God-given personal strengths, we find ourselves even better prepared for our successive chapters in life.

As we approach our forties, many of us begin to experience an unsettling sense of bewilderment. We wonder if all we have worked for will amount to much after we are gone. I (Nelson) used to work in research and development, improving old products and inventing new products in the plastics industry. I paused at one point to assess the lifecycle of the products in our company, and I observed that they were generally obsolete after four to five years. While this provided job security for those in new product development, I began to see that everything I was working on at the time would end up in the dustbin of corporate history in a short time.

Our fifties are marked by health and wisdom.

I was entering into a stage that most in their forties encounter—a phase that sociologists call *middlescence*. Our kids are nearly grown, we are at the top of our careers and we're left wondering if this is as good as it gets. Jim Conway brought focus to this phenomenon with his book, *Men in Midlife Crisis*. Bob Buford captured the practical issues of working through this life stage in his book, *Halftime*, and a series of books that followed. This is a time when we benefit by looking up from our desks and pausing to consider what we might do in the second half of our adult years. This can be, for many of us, a precious interlude, when we make genuine eye contact with God. *What is my life all about?* we ask Him. *What will You have me do next?* Bill Hybels in his book, *The Power of a Whisper*, calls this "holding hands with God." In being simply still, we may experience a new intimacy with the Almighty during this pause.

Then we come to our fifties, an age that, for the first time in several millennia of recorded history, is marked by health and wisdom; because of medical advances we have both relative youth and decades of experience. It is a remarkable time. But this is also the point at which we no longer count the years since birth, but rather the years we have left. We've discovered most of the things we're *not* good at. As a consequence, our life decisions at this stage often hit the bull's eye on the first try. We've learned to operate in our areas of strength and to manage our weaknesses by delegating tasks of lesser interest to others.

In our sixties—often earlier—we Westerners now have increased freedom to choose our pursuits. This is prime time. We can choose causes that will make a difference after we're gone. Or not. We can choose to make a difference at a time when making a bundle strangely loses its attraction. We can choose to change lives. Or we can choose to coast and simply change channels. And these choices—the physical, mental, emotional, spiritual and relational preparations we make in our sixties—will

> *We can choose to change lives or simply change channels.*

define our seventies and eighties, when our choices are gradually limited and eliminated by a myriad of health issues.

It's understandable if we run up against limitations due to the failure of our earthly bodies. But let it never be said that the reason we have little or nothing to show for our final decades is because we lacked spiritual fervor, that we failed to maximize the time and resources that were available to us in those years. This is the age when Moses was just getting started. The Lord used Moses, not in the strength of his youth, but when his youth was spent. And look what he accomplished by allowing the Lord to work through him. In the face of his example, we have no excuses for lamenting our limitations. For the first time in history, with such procedures as hip and knee replacements, we have more options than ever for extending our productive years.

Here's some good news, especially for those of us who look back on many decades of mistakes: The Lord miraculously works within our life choices. George Verwer, founder of Operation Mobilization, is fond of saying that the ideal is to go for Plan A. Often we mess up in life, forcing us to have to settle for Plan B. He admits to having messed up so many times that he is on Plan H. Then he quips, "I praise the Lord for a big alphabet."

Some, as they sense the curtain is near to closing, look back and recognize God's active, guiding hand involved in their life circumstances; they thank Him for never wasting an experience, for masterfully making the most of both their brokenness and their brilliance. They find themselves more and more empowered by God's incredible love, and they choose of their own free will—not as puppets on the Lord's strings—to pass on His love to others, even in their final breaths. Outwardly focused compassion seems, to them, a better choice than an inward focus on their own needs. They choose to become constructively employed by the Lord rather than wastefully consumed with self, even though the Lord grants them freedom to choose either.

What Can One Person Do?

But you may think, *The problems in my hometown, in my nation, in the world are too big for me to take on. There is too much need—too much corporate greed and government corruption, too much divorce, too many church splits, too many homeless, too many hungry and oppressed and impoverished. What can one person do?*

We are workers in the field; God produces the harvest.

We have an answer for that question: One person can operate by faith, by believing in a huge God who *will*, most assuredly, build His kingdom. One person can love people and make a difference in their lives. One person can take responsibility for behaving righteously and compassionately, knowing that it's God who takes responsibility for the results. We are workers in the field; God produces the harvest.

Jesus reinforced this truth throughout His teachings. He promised fruitful results for those individuals who invest their love and talents for Him—fruit that will far outweigh each person's effort. In the parable of the talents, Jesus voiced anger toward the servant who wasted his allotment by burying it "to keep it safe." That individual's meager "efforts" bore no fruit for the Lord, and so Jesus removed that man's reward.

The lone little boy in the crowd gave Jesus what he had—five loaves and two fish. And with that the Lord, the Multiplier, fed five thousand.

Or consider the personal promises implicit in Jesus' parables about seemingly small investments:

The kingdom of heaven is like a mustard seed, which a man took and sowed in his field, which indeed is the least of all the seeds; but when it is grown it is greater than the herbs and becomes a tree, so that the birds of the air come and nest in its branches. Another parable He spoke to them: The kingdom of heaven is like leaven, which a woman took and hid in three measures of meal till it was all leavened.

—Matthew 13: 31–33

Can you use your life to plant seeds and trust God for the outcome? Can you disciple a few and help them learn to disciple yet others? Can you trust God to use your life to make a God-sized impact, not just a you-sized impact? How big is your God?

Consider all the examples in Scripture of willing servants advancing the Lord's kingdom against impossible odds. Noah—one man with his family—built the ark by faith, and God used it to preserve humanity and all land-bound species of animal life. Abram left his home by faith, and believed God for a child in his old age, and through him the Lord founded a nation and inaugurated His salvation plan. Daniel and his friends, Shadrach, Meshach, and Abednego, on multiple occasions stood alone—stood firm—against a world power, under penalty of death. The number of lions in the den? Irrelevant. The temperature of the furnace? Immaterial. Because the Lord, not the servant, was in charge of the outcome.

Only humans are swayed by odds. God is never swayed.

Are you willing to follow the examples of Joshua, Gideon, David, Elisha and Hezekiah? They had their doubts, facing overwhelming opposing forces. But still they did their parts...and God did His. The odds didn't matter, because only humans are swayed by odds. God is never swayed, He's on your side, and He alone decides the outcome. You and the Lord are a majority!

You've been commissioned by your Commander in Chief to engage fully in battle. So fully armor up (Ephesians 6:10–20) and do for Him whatever you do best. When you're at your best, when you're feeling most energized, you are probably doing what the Lord designed you to do. What is His design for you? The purpose of this book is to help you make that discovery.

So let's move beyond the comfort of the armchair and get ready to launch into your journey. We're both here to coach you forward. Remember, you are not the first or even among the first thousand to tread this path. Many, many have gone before you. You're in good company as we set forth.

Chapter 2
Discerning Your Passion for Service

The great preacher Charles Spurgeon once said, "If you want to get people's attention, set yourself on fire and they will come to watch you burn." Your passion can remind others that they're only half-living, and can draw them toward God's truth, love and purpose.

Passion is a characteristic of a Jesus follower who feels strongly about correcting injustice, helping marginalized youth, bringing comfort to the lonely or even teaching principles of smart business to third-world entrepreneurs. Through most of this book we're going to use the word *passion* in a slightly different sense. When we speak of "your passion," we're referring to *the cause or topic* about which you think and feel passionately. One person's passion might be the need for greater community involvement within the members of your church, while another's might focus on tutoring learning-disabled children. Your personal passion could be any cause, program or campaign to promote justice, alleviate suffering, advance health, promote education, ensure safety, share the gospel, disciple the saints, stabilize church leaders or any combination of these and thousands of other causes.

Targeting your service toward your passion will infuse your ministry with zeal. That's why we encourage you to dream and stretch toward your passion, and we believe God wants you to let your passion be one of your guides in following your calling. Not your only guide, but one that can help you get halfway, helping you narrow the possible organizations you might work with, and ultimately identify the one that best embodies your passion in their mission and purpose.

Your passion, however, can offer only limited direction as you follow your calling; it can lead you to your team, but it can't define your specific role or duties; it can't pinpoint your job title in ministry. That aspect of your calling requires correct identification of your God-given talent strengths, which we'll examine in Chapters 3–6.

Zero-Percent Unemployment

Some people, despite their passion, believe they are simply too "normal" for ministry. George and Amy, for example. They felt inadequate because they were not Bible college graduates. George was a plumber, Amy was a homemaker, and although they felt a strong passion to serve overseas, they hesitated because they were uncertain how they could be used. *What*, they wondered, *could people with no ministry experience or theological training or cross cultural orientation possibly do in missions service?*

God answered their question when they attended a Finishers Forum conference. Numerous mission organizations were represented at the event, each clearly communicating their vision for feeding the hungry, for educating the poor, for translating the Bible, for teaching English as a second language. These agencies had come hundreds of miles, eagerly seeking any believers who were willing to give back to the Lord the hearts, skills, and resources He had given them. George and Amy received enthusiastic invitations from several organizations. "You're a homemaker and a plumber? We need hospitality people and maintenance people. We can use you!" The couple walked away—a little dazed—with a list of real, functioning organizations that had reached out to them and appeared to share George and Amy's passion. The agencies' representatives had identified several locations around the globe where the couple could serve with little or no special training. George and Amy had found

None of us gets a pass on the Great Commission.

their passion confirmed, and soon they would be living it out in life-impacting ministry.

None of us gets a pass on the Great Commission. None of us gets a pass on God's expectation of a fruitful life. Our Lord said, "Go." Get involved. Why do we stay put? All of us are called to contribute, each in our own unique way, to making reproducing disciples wherever the Lord puts us. George and Amy just had to make themselves available, to pursue their passion and to apply their God-given natural talents. They didn't have to reinvent themselves or go through extensive retraining. They accepted themselves as they were and offered the little they had back to the Lord. It became clear that He had accepted their offering with joy.

Okay, you respond, *but what about me? My work experience is restricted to a highly specialized field. Doesn't that limit my ministry potential?* Maybe you're a retired physicist, like our friend Harry from Canada. What did research into the atom have to contribute toward his passion for street children in Latin America? Harry found it easier to imagine what his wife, Sandra—a career nurse who had raised their family and was now taking classes toward a degree in counseling—could offer.

> *God is presenting an infinite variety of ways to share His love.*

Harry and Sandra participated in a consultation with mission agency executives. In one session they were invited to spend fifteen minutes telling their story to the audience of mission agency recruiters. Once the recruiters learned of the couple's spiritual maturity and strong desire to make a difference, each agency leader was able to recommend one or more places in their organization where they could make significant contributions in ministry service. The couple's past experience in no way limited their ability to pursue their present passion to serve using their occupational skills.

God is presenting an infinite variety of ways to share His love for others locally and globally—whether in Namibia or in your neighborhood. The myth is dying, that you have to be an evangelist to be a missionary or that you must have a seminary degree to touch lives around you. Jesus didn't say, "Go and evangelize the nations," but he did say, "Go and make disciples"—

If we pursue our passion, He'll make a way to multiply our efforts.

the word literally means "learners." People who pursue a passion in the context of a well-matched ministry organization can find a platform for some role in making disciples. Everyone has something to share.

Both of us have enjoyed the privilege of seeing the transformation, the dawning of hope, as people become aware how simple it can be to make a difference. "You mean," they marvel, "I can just bring myself and what little God has given me, and I can still have an eternal impact?" In fact, 1 Corinthians 1:26–31 says that God loves to powerfully use people that the rest of us would consider less than top-drawer. We've seen this happen over and over. God is more interested in our availability than our ability or occupational status. If we pursue our passion, He'll make a way to multiply our efforts.

Calling All Movers and Shakers

What if you're a successful, make-it-happen person? Maybe all of your efforts to date have been invested in being an entrepreneur or a business executive, and you think that no ministry opportunity exists for you. We've got a news bulletin for you! There are a myriad Christian service organizations that would happily ask you to help educate eager entrepreneurs in India or Afghanistan or other developing nations, perhaps by starting a new business education program for college-age students. Or maybe they'll urge you to help start a new radio station, develop an outward bound wilderness program for troubled teens, or open a medical supply warehouse. And these are just a few of the countless possible endeavors that would both take advantage of your experience and allow you to pursue your heart's passion to make an eternal difference. Working through this book will guide you toward a ministry role that is surprisingly well suited to you.

Here's another important observation: If you want to pursue your passion in other countries, the people there don't want you to come in and conduct the business, or set up the school, or run the government agency. They want to learn how *they* can do the job. If you're a mover and shaker, you can multiply yourself many times over by serving as a trainer or consultant, perhaps in numerous locations during your ministry tenure. (And, of course, such training and consulting roles are available in ministries on this side of the ocean, too.)

You don't have to be a highly trained business or administrative expert; many nationals in other countries have only a rudimentary understanding of business principles. You offer a wealth of experience if you can coach them in basic business planning, how to write up a proposal, or how to establish an orphanage. Anyone with any kind of government experience (who, for example, has served an unpaid internship), or who has done volunteer ministry at home, or who has served in any type of leadership role can make a difference. The world respects the success of Westerners. They want to listen. And then *they* want to get to work implementing what they've learned from you.

What If the Thrill Is Gone?

You may be thinking, *I don't feel passionate about anything these days. So how can I expect to find my personal passion?*

We are made in the image of a God of emotions, and He has designed us to feel strongly. But we sometimes use defensive strategies to dampen the highs and lows of our feelings. Or, by choice or by force of circumstances, we may have had limited exposure to those aspects of the world that would stir strong feelings in our hearts. In the words of Lloyd Reeb, spokesman for Halftime,

> *We are made in the image of a God of emotions.*

Faced with obligations and responsibility, we may have turned our "dreamer" off decades ago. Finding our passion is about learning to listen to our heart, and we may need to relearn that skill.... Our passion may be hidden in plain view—so we may simply need others around to help us see it.... We may have been so focused on one niche that we have little exposure to the wide array of needs and opportunities out there.

Reeb clarifies another strategy we can use to discern our personal passion: "Our deepest passion may be around what we can bring to an issue or a cause rather than a specific cause itself." We have a need to be needed, to make a contribution of significance. If nothing else helps you find your passion, you might ask yourself, *What do I have to offer? And where can I get excited about using it?*

Or perhaps you need to address an even more fundamental issue—your basic attitude about service. Maybe your first step—even before identifying your specific passion or your talent strengths—is to make a purposeful, conscious decision: *Will I choose to love others as much as I love myself? Will I bring my talents, passion, training and experience to express my love for others? Will I surrender my brilliance and my brokenness to God?*

This decision won't make itself. You must consciously determine: *I'll spend my years loving others rather than being consumed with myself.* If you've already been living with this attitude, then you already know the immense joy that comes with genuine service to God and others. And if you're just now discovering a servant's heart, we promise you won't regret the decision to serve.

You're about to launch into three exercises that will guide you through the discernment of your personal passion and the beginnings of identifying your possible team. But first take a minute to submit your passion and skills to the King of the universe. Ask Him to release His love for others so that it flows through you and through all that you bring, for His pleasure.

> *Dear Father, I submit to You all of my desires, my dreams and my aptitudes. I seek Your glory and wish to serve in whatever way pleases You. Thank You for allowing me the opportunity to love others as You have loved me. Amen*

Exercise One
Discerning Your Personal Passion

The Bible gives examples of individuals whose hearts are stirred for service to God. This stirring usually results in action and serves as a strong indicator of one's passion. Often passion comes to the surface when we feel drawn to a need or observe an injustice. Other times we read a book or listen to a sermon and are moved to action. (Please understand that all exercises in this book are copyrighted and should not be copied.)

Three Favorite Classes or Activities
Use the list below to prompt your memory of subjects that stirred and excited you in high school and college. In which classes were you particularly eager to pursue a special project or task? In the spaces provided below the checklist, write your most enjoyed classes.

- ❏ Art, design
- ❏ Astronomy
- ❏ Bible
- ❏ Business
- ❏ Communication
- ❏ Computer science
- ❏ Culinary arts
- ❏ Drama
- ❏ Economics
- ❏ Education
- ❏ Engineering
- ❏ English, literature
- ❏ Environmental science
- ❏ Fashion
- ❏ Finance, accounting
- ❏ General sciences
- ❏ Geography
- ❏ Health sciences
- ❏ History
- ❏ International relations
- ❏ Journalism
- ❏ Lab sciences
- ❏ Languages
- ❏ Law
- ❏ Law enforcement
- ❏ Marine sciences
- ❏ Math
- ❏ Media, film
- ❏ Medicine
- ❏ Wildlife management
- ❏ Military science
- ❏ Music
- ❏ Nutrition
- ❏ Philosophy
- ❏ Photography
- ❏ Physical education
- ❏ Political science
- ❏ Psychology
- ❏ Recreation
- ❏ Shop
- ❏ Social science
- ❏ Speech, debate
- ❏ Textiles
- ❏ Theology
- ❏ Transportation
- ❏ Veterinary sciences

Three high school or college classes or activities that stirred and excited you most:

1. _____ Why? _____

2. _____ Why? _____

3. _____ Why? _____

Three Books or Articles
Name three recent books or articles (maybe on the Web) that piqued your interest:

1. _____ Why? _____

2. _____ Why? _____

3. _____ Why? _____

Three Sermons
God can speak to your heart through a message or sermon. Write down three sermons, chapel messages or retreat talks that recently inspired you:

1.Message theme: _____

2.Message theme: _____

3.Message theme: _____

Three Bible Verses
God will use His Word to awaken our passions. Choose three Bible verses that have recently inspired you:

1. _____

2. _____

3. _____

Three Bible or Historical Characters
Notable men and women may rouse our hearts, especially in the areas of our passions. Choose three characters from the Bible or history who have recently inspired you:

1. _____ Why? _____

2. _____ Why? _____

3. _____ Why? _____

Exercise Two
Your Passion Checklist

We can be moved to act when reading the news, taking a short-tem missions trip or hearing the cry of a person in trouble. Use the following checklist to recall issues or causes that have roused your passion.

MINISTRY TOPICS
- ❏ Aid for foreign national business startups
- ❏ Art in ministry
- ❏ Business ethics
- ❏ Church in local culture
- ❏ Drug/alcohol abuse
- ❏ Education
- ❏ Evangelism
- ❏ Family debt
- ❏ Government, judicial policy
- ❏ Handicapped, disabled
- ❏ Health care, nutrition
- ❏ Homeless, hungry
- ❏ Homeless youth
- ❏ Legal help
- ❏ Marriage, family
- ❏ Media
- ❏ Morality in sports, entertainment
- ❏ Political elections
- ❏ Poor
- ❏ Pornography, gambling
- ❏ Prayer outreach
- ❏ Prison ministry
- ❏ Public policy
- ❏ Racial reconciliation
- ❏ Refugees, immigrants
- ❏ Sanctity of life
- ❏ Senior citizen
- ❏ Undernourished children
- ❏ Youth slave trafficking

WORLD REGIONS
- ❏ Central America
- ❏ Eastern Europe
- ❏ Europe
- ❏ India Subcontinent
- ❏ Middle East, North Africa
- ❏ North America
- ❏ Pacific Rim
- ❏ Russia, Central Asia
- ❏ South America
- ❏ Southeast Asia
- ❏ Sub-Sahara Africa

LANGUAGES
- ❏ English as a native language
- ❏ English as a second language
- ❏ Spanish
- ❏ French
- ❏ German
- ❏ Another European language
- ❏ Portuguese
- ❏ Russian
- ❏ Japanese
- ❏ Arabic
- ❏ Mandarin
- ❏ Korean
- ❏ An Indian language
- ❏ An African language
- ❏ Another Asian language
- ❏ Other

RELIGION GROUPS

- ❏ Animist
- ❏ Buddhist
- ❏ Confucianist
- ❏ Hindu
- ❏ Jewish
- ❏ Muslim
- ❏ Sikh
- ❏ Christian
- ❏ Cults
- ❏ Pseudo Christian groups: Mormon, New Age, Jehovah's Witnesses

PEOPLE GROUPS

- ❏ Adults, addictive behavior
- ❏ Adults, career 30–45
- ❏ Adults, college
- ❏ Adults, dementia
- ❏ Adults, divorce care
- ❏ Adults, executives
- ❏ Adults, homeless
- ❏ Adults, loss of child
- ❏ Adults, loss of job
- ❏ Adults, loss of spouse
- ❏ Adults, men
- ❏ Adults, mentally challenged
- ❏ Adults, midlife 45–65
- ❏ Adults, physically challenged
- ❏ Adults, prisoners
- ❏ Adults, seniors
- ❏ Adults, women
- ❏ Adults, young 20–30
- ❏ Artists
- ❏ Care, HIV, AIDS
- ❏ Children, at risk
- ❏ Children, grades K–5
- ❏ Children, grades 6–12
- ❏ Children, mentally challenged
- ❏ Children, physically challenged
- ❏ Children, preschool
- ❏ Children of prisoners
- ❏ Christian, adults
- ❏ Christian, school age
- ❏ Christian, seniors
- ❏ Christian, teens
- ❏ Christian young adults
- ❏ Chronically ill
- ❏ College, international students
- ❏ College students
- ❏ Fathers
- ❏ Graduated care residents
- ❏ Illiterate
- ❏ Immigrants
- ❏ Law enforcement
- ❏ Married, abused
- ❏ Married, couples
- ❏ Married, dying spouse
- ❏ Military
- ❏ Mothers
- ❏ Mothers, preschoolers
- ❏ Mothers, single parents
- ❏ Mothers, unwed
- ❏ Musicians
- ❏ Refugees
- ❏ Rescue
- ❏ Shut-ins
- ❏ U.S. minority groups
- ❏ Welfare recipients
- ❏ Youth, addictive behavior
- ❏ Youth, delinquent
- ❏ Youth, homeless
- ❏ Youth, middle & high school
- ❏ Youth, street kids

From the list above, note your selections of greatest interest:

Ministry Topics _____

World Regions_____

Languages _____

Religion Groups_____

People Groups_____

Passion Statements
Use your self-insights from Exercises One and Two to complete the following statements.

As I consider desperate needs—needs in my church, needs in my community and needs in the world...

a. I have always had a special interest in_____

_____

b. I feel God is leading me to _____

_____

c. Someone should do something about_____

_____

d. It really gets me upset when I hear about_____

_____

e. I feel that I am doing something significant when I_____

_____

f. If there was some way, I would like to help others by_____

_____

Exercise Three
First Steps for Finding the Team

Exercises One and Two have helped you discern your personal passion. Now it's time to use the self-insights you've gained to begin identifying the types of ministry organizations that most likely share your passion for service. Use the lists of church, local and global ministries below to make your selections. More extensive lists are available in Exercise Ten (Chapter 7) and links to Internet lists of ministry organizations are provided in Exercise Eleven (Chapter 8). At this stage, we're only narrowing down to broad categories of ministries. Later we'll guide you through the steps of naming specific local or global organizations.

1. Church-Related Ministries. Below are listed typical church ministry departments, as well as new church plants. Consider your responses in Exercises One and Two as you select the church-related ministries that appear to share your passion for service. (Exercise Ten, at the end of Chapter 7, provides a more specific list of church departments and projects.) Enter your selections in the table on the last page of this chapter.

❏ Church support services
❏ Church counseling, care giving
❏ Church evangelism, outreach
❏ Church leadership, management
❏ Church music, art, drama

❏ Church operations, facilities
❏ Church recreation, events
❏ Church teaching, discipleship
❏ New church plants

2. Local and Global Ministry Organizations. Select one or more ministry organization categories. (Refer to Exercise Ten, at the end of Chapter 7, for a more detailed list, as well as the appropriate CONI numbers. The CONI, or Christian Organization Numerical Index, numbers will help when you use online databases for seeking out specific ministries.) Enter your selections in the table on last page of this chapter.

❏ Advertising, arts & cultural organizations
❏ Advocacy, human rights & political organizations
❏ Agriculture & livestock support organizations

❏ Children services & outreach organizations
❏ Church, church consulting & support organizations
❏ Community development, construction & maintenance orgs.

- ❑ Computer & related technology service organizations
- ❑ Consulting & legal services organizations
- ❑ Counseling, residential recovery organizations
- ❑ Crisis intervention & disaster relief organizations
- ❑ Disabled services, outreach organizations
- ❑ Discipleship & prayer organizations
- ❑ Distribution service organizations
- ❑ Education & literacy organizations
- ❑ Employment mobilization, referral organizations
- ❑ Evangelism organizations
- ❑ Family & marriage concerns organizations
- ❑ Financial aid & business development organizations
- ❑ Foundations, trusts & membership organizations
- ❑ Hospitality, boarding service organizations
- ❑ Immigrant & refugee service organizations
- ❑ Jail & prison outreach organizations
- ❑ Marketplace outreach organizations
- ❑ Mechanical & technical repair organizations
- ❑ Media, broadcasting & publicity organizations
- ❑ Medical, dental & health service organizations
- ❑ Men's concerns organizations
- ❑ Music & drama organizations
- ❑ Publishing & printing organizations
- ❑ Recovery, rehab & reconciliation organizations
- ❑ Research, archaeology & translation organizations
- ❑ Seniors, retirement organizations
- ❑ Sports & recreation organizations
- ❑ Stores: book, thrift, catalog, specialty
- ❑ Transportation service organizations
- ❑ Women's concerns organizations

List three to five selections here from the church, local and global ministry organization categories:

Ministry Organization Categories	Optional: CONI Number from Exercise Ten

Congratulations. You have identified several types of ministry organizations which represent your passion for service. Next, in Chapters 3–6 you will learn the best job titles (job duties) in those organizations which match your God-given talent strengths.

Chapter 3
Discovering Your *Communicational* Talent Strengths

We're now ready to explore your God-given talents. Since 1973, I (John), along with a team of others, have been studying natural talents to determine those that are truly God-given, as opposed to those that can be acquired by hard work or education. Through a process that has involved three doctoral dissertations, we have identified and validated a total of fifty-four natural talents in three categories: *Communicational* talents, *Relational* talents and *Functional* talents. We're going to take the next three chapters to help you understand these and determine which are yours. We begin in this chapter with *Communicational* talents.

We tend to divide people into two categories: "good communicators" (salesmen, marketers, politicians, teachers and others who are good with words) and "not-good communicators" (mechanics, accountants, homemakers, bus drivers and others who are not typically as good with words). But in Scripture, God indicates that He has created *all* people to be good communicators, if for no other reason than that all are called to communicate their faith. But not everyone communicates in the same way, and we tend to overlook some of the most powerful modes of expression at our disposal. Over the past thirty-plus years, my team's research efforts have analyzed over ninety thousand career options—all with a view to distinguishing innate, God-given traits. In the *Communicational* category my colleagues and I have identified fifteen natural talents, each with its own distinctive mode of expression. Every human—yes, everyone—has at least one best *Communicational* strength by which he or she expresses his or her most sincere feelings and convictions. These fifteen talents are listed and defined in Exercise Five, at the end of this chapter, which you will use to determine your own *Communicational* talents.

Everyone has at least one best Communicational strength.

In every area of life—especially in our ministry service roles, where we communicate eternal truths to make an eternal impact—it makes sense that we communicate best when we do it according to the way God has wired us individually. Our God-given *Communicational* talent or talents are the means by which we present ourselves most naturally, confidently and authentically. We may be able to attain adequacy when using communication methods that are not natural strengths, but we risk coming across as stressed or phony. So discovering one's natural *Communicational* talent is important.

You say you experience stage fright? Public speaking makes your knees knock? Take courage. By God's design, you are still a communicator. That doesn't mean you must be talented at *Giving Speeches or Sermons* (Talent 3, below). You have fourteen other *Communicational* strengths that might be yours. When you discover your best *Communicational* talent or talents, you will open doorways for conveying the gospel and other biblical truth—doorways that are especially designed for you, through which few other people could "speak" into the lives of others. Public speaking is not the top of the communication totem pole.

We don't have space in this chapter to fully develop and discuss all fifteen *Communicational* talents, but we will highlight several of the most unexpected and the most misunderstood.

The Greatest Story Ever Sewn

Marge (Nelson's wife) is an artist—an artist in fabrics and thread. She spends hours pouring over Scripture, mining God's

Word for its rich visual imagery, especially in the Old Testament and in Jesus' parables. Then she creates quilts emblazoned with collages of the Bible's images, by which she can then communicate biblical ideas. Her work has a way of grasping attention and imparting God's truth, often with amazing detail. Insight without words.

One quilt depicts the story of Genesis 1—a visual description of the six days of creation. Marge once took the quilt to a cultural exchange festival in an oppressed Asian country where it was displayed in a public area. This was not a Christian event, and yet Marge was free to explain to viewers the meaning of the images, using the quilt as her text.

When the nationals spoke to each other in their language, it was impossible for Marge's group to follow the conversations, but there was no mistaking—from body language and tones of voice—the gist of the dialog. A translator reported that some onlookers were objecting: "We don't believe in a God who created us. We believe that we determine our own outcomes and that man is supreme." But the hearts and minds of other nationals were moved because the artistry conveyed not only ideas, but also emotion in the beauty of God's handiwork and His loving care for His creation.

There was another unexpected outcome. Since Bibles are not readily available in this country, local believers memorize large portions of Scripture and carry God's Word in their hearts and minds. Believers at the festival engaged in conversation with other nationals, quoting Genesis 1 from memory as prompted by the images designed into the quilt. In this way the Lord used the quilt as a focal point for conversations between Christ-followers and skeptics.

Marge is gifted at communicating through two natural talents—namely, *Designing* and *Using Shapes and Forms* (Talents 6 and 9, below). Similarly, God has gifted you with at least one best *Communicational* talent, and you will express yourself most confidently and authentically using it as you impart the truth of His love to others. Any way you can think to convey scriptural reality—using the form or forms of communication with which God has specially gifted you—the Holy Spirit can use your efforts to communicate love and to change lives.

Any way you can think to communicate, the Holy Spirit can use it.

On another occasion, Marge visited a village in Central Asia, in one of the many 'stan countries of the former Soviet Union. The local missionaries had worked with the people for five years with little result, even though the nationals demonstrated belief in the spiritual realm through their superstitions. But when the nonverbal creation quilt was displayed, these people suddenly had questions about God, life and the Bible. The locals told the missionaries, "Oh! We didn't know you interested in spiritual things." They responded to the visual message because they were not threatened by a quilt—they didn't feel preached at. Marge and the other believers simply explained the artwork and the related biblical themes—informing while entertaining.

In addition to the creation quilt, Marge took along a quilt that depicted the Lord's segregating of the sheep and the goats in Matthew 25 :31–46. The sheep and goats passed through a bloodstained doorway. The goats that had reached their destination, near the bottom of the quilt, were shown in isolation, each separated from the others. The sheep, on the other hand, were shown living in community, making their way together upward into the clouds on a path of golden thread.

Music can help people voice their emotions toward God.

The villagers had never received any teaching of the Bible's content, but now Jesus' teaching from Matthew 25 was depicted visually before them. The people raised questions, allowing the Western workers to articulate a portion of God's Word using a visual *Communicational* style where conversation alone had previously failed. The experience made an amazingly powerful impact on the people.

We too often miss out on "languages" that we don't even know are available—languages that some individuals and cultures "speak" fluently, and through which they are most receptive.

You're Singing Our Language!

Some cultures have proven resistant to the written word simply because they have never communicated by means of writing. Even when missionaries and other educators create a written form to match the locals' spoken language, it takes time for minds to transition from a centuries-long heritage of oral communication to the new mode of written-word communication. During this transition period, the most effective methods for conveying God's truth and love make use of nontraditional *Communicational* talents.

Some specialists have broken through to such cultures by applying their gifting and experience in the field of ethnomusicology—putting biblical principles into a musical style that is native to the people, and in their native tongue. Eskimos, for example, have become overjoyed to learn that they can express their hearts and worship God, not only with language, but in their own familiar artistic style. Their music has conditioned them from infancy, and this art form can elicit associated emotions and help the people voice those emotions toward God. The world needs skilled musicians (see Talents 11 and 14, below).

New discoveries in Bible translation find that to educate a native group in the Scriptures works best when the Bible is communicated in oral and dramatized story format first, before a written text is prepared. What is more, this method of Bible teaching is not a monopoly of those distant cultures; it works great here in our homes and neighborhoods, too. Who would ever have guessed that parents who discovered they were gifted at telling stories to their children might some day end up sharing the gospel with that same storytelling energy to an unreached people group. And no, seminaries don't typically offer Storytelling 101.

Where No (White) Man Made Sense Before

Jens and his wife were missionaries in North Africa. She was a doctor who served in a mission hospital serving poor nationals. Jens was an artist working out of a forty-foot box trailer as his studio. He spent a year observing and learning the communication style, culture and thought patterns of the nationals. This culture had no pictorial language and no art forms other than body art. After a year, Jens used what he had learned to begin creating abstract drawings of the cross and other elements from Scripture. The local people were fascinated and entered into dialogue about God, His Word and biblical living. This opened the door for Jens to explain the gospel by explaining the art. His understanding of their culture and communication style was so captivating that he was invited to appear on national TV. He was also invited to the president's palace.

Jens was proving that listening is half of communication.

Other missionaries looked at Jens's drawings and couldn't make heads or tails of them. Meanwhile, Jens led a number of people to a personal relationship with the Lord and started a church.

That first year, when Jens set aside his usual work and studied the local people, might appear to some observers to be "a year off." But far from loafing, Jens was working hard, proving that listening is half of communication. He was practicing the principals of being slow to speak and quick to listen (see James

1:19). Once he understood the communication styles of his audience, he was able to "speak" more effectively than if he had started immediately using traditional methods that had failed for decades.

Misguided Communicational Zeal

One of the talents most sought after by those wanting to pursue ministry service is *Teaching* (Talent 4, below). Men and women often state that they want to serve God by teaching those who are less fortunate, who need basic health skills, who need a chance to rise above the poverty level, who need basic business training, and even those who are not succeeding in mainsteam US public education. However, it's one thing to possess the natural, God-given talent of *Teaching* and quite another to fulfill the job duty of teaching. Much confusion can be avoided—and much otherwise disappointed zeal can be put to productive use—by simply clarifying the difference between the *Teaching* gift and the teaching role.

Frank was an example of a zealous, would-be teacher. He couldn't stop thinking about it. He worked with computers as an electrical engineer, but didn't feel that his work contributed to God's kingdom. So he quit his job to enroll in a master's-level teaching program, then went to teach children in Africa.

It's one thing to have the Teaching talent and another to fulfill the job.

Two years later, disillusioned by his poor performance in the classroom, Frank was back in his home city, making a living as a computer consultant. His African teaching endeavor had failed.

That's when he came to my (John's) office asking for assistance. When I sat down with Frank to discuss his profile of natural talent strengths, he was surprised to find that the natural talent for *Teaching*—lecturing in a traditional classroom setting with limited audience interaction—did not show up as one of his strengths. We discussed this at length. Frank, understandably, wondered why he would have such a strong zeal for teaching when *Teaching* did not show up in his test results. Surely the test had to be wrong. How could God give him such a strong motivation for this pursuit and not also give him the aptitude to fulfill it?

We then explored the *Communicational* talents that did show as Frank's strengths. The top one was *Conversing*—that is, communicating face to face with one or two others (Talent 2, below). Frank had not considered the possibility that the role of teacher might employ any talent other than *Teaching*. He assumed that the activity of teaching could only be done in the classroom—or at least in some setting with a teacher in front and students seated in their chairs. He thought of everyday conversing as something totally separate, inappropriate for the task of teaching.

Conversing is the most common Communicational talent strength.

Frank had also discovered that he was drawn to children with some type of learning disability. In fact, his *Conversing* talent fit perfectly with one-on-one interactive instruction to help learning disabled children. So, instead of classroom teaching, now Frank found that he could teach one-to-one. His yearning to teach was fulfilled. This realization changed everything for Frank, and he pursued a career as a speech therapist specializing in children.

Frank was finally convinced that God had gifted him appropriately for a special purpose, to fulfill his perfect role in God's plan. He didn't have to twist and force himself into a mismatched role. He correctly reinterpreted his God-given makeup and redirected his zeal toward a service goal that was more consistent with his wiring.

Frank is not alone. Research shows that *Conversing* is the most common *Communicational* talent strength out of all fifteen, so a surprisingly large number of people should be looking for ways to pursue their passion through the use of this talent. If *Conversing* stands out as your one primary *Communicational* talent, you should shape your job description to spend at least 60 percent of your work hours communicating face to face, rather than by telephone, e-mail, Skype, classroom instruction or leading small groups. This *Conversing* talent would be suited to such teaching roles as one-on-one discipling, mentoring, coaching, consulting or counseling.

To further illustrate the variety of natural talents that can prove useful in the activity of teaching, let's set aside the largest portion of the teaching pie (including roles that involve teaching individually, in small groups, by audio or video recording, by live broadcast, by telephone or live web chat, and so on), and let's consider six talents that empower a person to be at their best in an up-front teaching role. We call these the "platform" talents, and they are *Giving Speeches or Sermons* (often referred to as preaching or public speaking), *Teaching, Acting or Imitating Mannerisms, Facilitating Group Discussion, Singing or Instrument Playing* and *Giving Presentations* (Talents 3–4 and 12–15, below). A person might sense one or more of these strengths in himself, correctly interpret it as a talent for teaching, and then incorrectly proceed to pursue a ministry position in classroom teaching. Each of these platform talents operates best in its own cluster of learning environments, not necessarily in the traditional classroom.

Identify your innate talent before selecting your best job position.

When searching for your best ministry fit, it is important to first identify your innate talent (for example, *Facilitating Group Discussion*) before selecting your best role or job position (for example, classroom teacher or one-on-one consultant). Then, equipped with this understanding of your natural talents and your ideal job description, you can approach ministry organizations that share your passion, and you can ask, "In what job can I serve, using my *Communicational* talent strength of _____?" (You fill the blank.)

Communication by Imitation

One of my (John's) favorite *Communicational* talents is *Acting or Imitating Mannerisms* (Talent 12, below). This is also one of the most misunderstood and underestimated of all fifty-four talents. Think about the following people you know, who are not professional actors, yet have touched your life: your favorite school teacher, your favorite storyteller, your favorite camp counselor, your favorite sales person, your favorite counselor or therapist, and your favorite pastor or preacher. All of these individuals have something in common—a generous dose of God-given *Acting* talent. They are able to observe and identify with you closely. Using their perceptiveness, they can unconsciously put on different hats and speak and act in a way that best addresses your need. If appropriate, they may even become like you in body language, speech mannerisms and other ways that set you at ease and help you trust them.

What is more, successful missionaries point to a key *Acting*-related trait that predicts whether or not a new missionary will succeed in a new assignment. That trait is how well the person adapts to the new culture—how well he or she fits in. I remember a cross-cultural experience in high school: I was selected, as one of twelve US high school students, to represent my school for a summer program in Mexico, where I would live with a family in their home. My host family had a high school-age son, Chico, and one of the activities I enjoyed most was hanging out with Chico and other boys our age. Chico and I went everywhere together; I even attended class with him on occasion. We did his job together, passing out leaflets to local businesses. We went to parties together and talked about all the girls. I learned how to dance and bought special boots for flamenco-style foot stomping. I even learned several Mexican songs on my guitar and still to this day can sing "Happy Birthday" in Spanish.

One day I was horsing around with Chico and his friends when one of them, Bernardo, said, "Hey Juan [that's me], you aren't like the others, the gringos. You are one of us."

An Acting-related trait predicts whether a missionary will succeed.

I smiled and said, "Gracias," not fully understanding what he meant. I now realize that he was saying, "We accept you. You are real to us. You don't stick out like a sore thumb." Yes, I had noticed that my US colleagues spoke Spanish with a Yankee accent and at times seemed wooden and uncomfortable. But I had not considered how that would make a difference in their relationships with the local youth.

It turned out that I was the only one in the group who had made genuine friends with the Mexican boys and girls. To me it was just natural fun; I wasn't consciously trying to be anything but myself. But unconsciously, I was a cultural chameleon. That's how I discovered that I have some *Acting* in my blood. It especially comes alive when you put me in a cross-cultural environment, where I watch carefully what the locals do and then imitate them. After all, that is what movie actors do—they study a particular character and then imitate him or her so carefully that you, the film viewer, believe that the actor is truly the character.

Now, did I say that any person aspiring to disciple, teach or evangelize cross-culturally should have an *Acting* talent? No. But having this talent does speed up a person's acclimation and help them avoid ostracism because they're different. And cross-cultural ministry is only one of many ministry categories in which the *Acting* talent be of significant benefit. Whether it is in discipleship, consulting, teaching, counseling, leading worship, preaching, or one of many other ministry roles—if the job requires interaction with other people, the *Acting* talent can make a big difference in performance outcomes.

Begin Your Self-Discovery

The real-life examples in this chapter document the fact that nontraditional modes of communication—visual arts, performing arts, music, and more—can be used to make a difference, sometimes where nothing else will work. We don't have to be verbal communicators, such as evangelists, writers, teachers, preachers or discussion group leaders, to be effective where the Lord puts us. God has wired each of us with at least one best *Communicational* talent, by which to share truth and compassion for others in an authentic way.

We don't have to be verbal communicators to be effective.

Now let's begin the discovery process for identifying the ways God has gifted you to communicate. We will do this in two steps. First, you will conduct a quick review of your life's enjoyable experiences in Exercise Four. This is a short trip down memory lane to jog your recollection of home activities, hobbies, enjoyable school activities and even enjoyable work activities, if applicable. You will recognize some items repeated from Exercise Two. But this time you're considering them from a different angle. Rather than asking whether your passion is stirred by these topics or issues, this time you are taking the first step of a four-exercise process (Chapters 3–5), probing into the talents you used most often while doing those activities. Exercise Four will result in a list of your ten most enjoyable activities since high school. You'll keep these activities in mind as you move on to the second step (Exercise Five), a talent assessment survey, to evaluate your *Communicational* strength or strengths.

Research has shown that the activities you enjoy—especially hobbies, vacations, pastimes and volunteer experiences—best define your innate talents. Your work, home responsibilities and church life may or may not provide the opportunity for your application of a talent strength; you may see few if any specific talents stand out consistently among these "obligatory" activities. But a number of talents can emerge, popping up time after time, as you examine several of the "non-obligatory" activities—hobbies and pastimes you've enjoyed. So we'll focus on your most fun activities in identifying your natural talents.

Activities you enjoy best define your innate talents.

For example, *Using Handcrafts* (Talent 10, below) is used in building models, stringing beads, needlepoint, making jewelry, wood carving and metal engraving, among other activities. Only a small number of people with this talent actually use it on the job or regularly for home chores or church responsibilities. But many who possess this gifting find expression for it in their hobbies and volunteer activities. Nor is this a trivial talent. A person gifted this way in the Old Testament times would have been a candidate for the tabernacle embroidery or inlay tooling work. Today, there are multiple applications for this talent in reaching out to children, to the elderly and those suffering from stroke or accident (through occupational and art therapy), and to those in long-term care facilities. The *Using Handcrafts* talent opens unexpected doors for communicating love and compassion where words cannot do the job. Participants tend to develop special bonds, which can then lead to opportunities to express one's faith with authenticity. If you possess this talent, you might never think to apply it in ministry unless you looked to your leisure activities to discover your natural talents.

Exercise Four
Your Enjoyable Life Experiences Checklist

Remember those special times in your life when you were in your prime, when one of your priorities was simply having a good time? It might have been a good time at work or at play, at school or in church, with people or on your own. Wherever it was, you were having fun.

We have developed the following list to help you revisit past enjoyable experiences and activities from your freshman year of high school to the present. Review this list and place a check by each activity you have enjoyed. Whether you received any recognition or award is not the point. The question is, Did you enjoy it? You may have only engaged in an activity briefly, but remember it as a great experience, though short-lived. Check it. This is as important as long sustained experiences you've enjoyed over months and years.

HOBBIES, LEISURE ACTIVITIES
- ❏ Photography
- ❏ Building models
- ❏ Designing clothing
- ❏ Sewing
- ❏ Needlework
- ❏ Interior decorating
- ❏ Gardening, lawn care
- ❏ Flower arranging
- ❏ Fine arts, painting
- ❏ Sculpting
- ❏ Cooking
- ❏ Reading
- ❏ Creative writing
- ❏ Speaking to groups
- ❏ Short wave radio, CB
- ❏ Electronics
- ❏ Metalworking, jewelry
- ❏ Home remodeling
- ❏ Construction
- ❏ Car repair
- ❏ Arts, Crafts
- ❏ Games: chess, bridge, Monopoly, etc.
- ❏ Sports
- ❏ Collecting things
- ❏ Traveling
- ❏ Antiques
- ❏ Woodworking
- ❏ Crossword puzzles
- ❏ Word games
- ❏ Camping, hiking, backpacking
- ❏ Hunting, fishing, trapping
- ❏ Discussion groups
- ❏ Concerts: symphony, jazz, rock
- ❏ Volunteer teaching
- ❏ Driving & operating vehicles: auto, motorcycle, etc.
- ❏ Pets: fish, cat, dog
- ❏ Ceramics, leather tooling
- ❏ Read business magazines
- ❏ Political campaigns
- ❏ Attend auctions, sales
- ❏ Teacher's aid, tutor
- ❏ Write letters to publications
- ❏ Art galleries, exhibits
- ❏ Play on team, athletic activities
- ❏ Cut friends' hair, apply makeup

- Serve food at receptions
- Member of music group (folk, country, etc.)
- Boating
- Flying
- Horseback riding
- Upholstering
- Make posters for activity
- Dramatic performance
- Member of a study group
- Individual study & research of a topic
- Movie, films
- Writing literary material
- Singing as performer
- Playing musical instrument
- Conducting music
- Writing music
- Chemistry experiments
- Time with family, friends
- Appliance repair
- Listening to friends (counseling)
- Rearranging home, furniture
- Budgeting finances, checkbook
- Researching a subject
- Coaching a team
- Arranging social gathering
- Computer work
- Attending plays, drama
- Acting in dramatic group
- Dancing: social, ballet, jazz, etc.
- Promoting group activities
- Graphic design, cartoons, signs
- Watching TV
- Entertaining guests
- Dabbling in stocks, investments, real estate
- Bargaining ("swapping")
- Exercising
- Computer games, video games
- Other _____

COMMUNITY ACTIVITIES
- Service clubs, etc.
- Junior chamber of commerce
- Civic volunteer
- Head Start, etc.
- United Way, March of Dimes
- Neighborhood groups
- Political campaigns
- Parent-teacher association
- Christian business clubs
- Civil Air Patrol
- Environmental group
- Consumer group
- Hospital volunteer
- Museum, historical society
- Scouting troop
- Rescue squad, volunteer fire department
- Fundraising activities
- Care for shut-ins
- Other _____

SCHOOL ACTIVITIES, SUBJECTS
- Future Farmers of America, 4H
- Foreign exchange student
- Student government
- Athletics: individual, team
- Cheerleader, pep squad
- Drama, theatre
- Orchestra, band
- Boy Scouts, Girl Scouts
- Chorus
- Christian campus clubs
- Political clubs
- Social concern projects
- Sorority, fraternity
- Dormitory offices
- Debate team
- Auto, motorcycle, agricultural mechanics
- Chemistry
- Language
- Art
- Business
- Science club
- Chess club
- Future teachers
- Journalism

- ❏ Library
- ❏ Math
- ❏ Photography
- ❏ Safety patrol
- ❏ School newspaper
- ❏ Speech club
- ❏ Yearbook staff
- ❏ Building trades
- ❏ Radio broadcasting
- ❏ Home economics
- ❏ Industrial arts
- ❏ Other _____

CHURCH ACTIVITIES
- ❏ Missionary benefits
- ❏ Evangelism
- ❏ Organized social activities

- ❏ Nursery
- ❏ Choir, special music, tours
- ❏ Visitation
- ❏ Master of ceremonies
- ❏ Bible studies
- ❏ Youth groups
- ❏ Sunday school classes
- ❏ Conferences, retreats
- ❏ Board memberships
- ❏ Trustee
- ❏ Teaching classes
- ❏ Special committees
- ❏ Summer programs
- ❏ Camp programs
- ❏ Discipline
- ❏ Other _____

List other experiences you have enjoyed.

Enjoyable work experiences, if applicable:

Other experiences, hobbies and activities you have enjoyed:

Your Top Ten
To help you recognize the talent-threads woven through and connecting the different activities of your life, circle the ten (no more than twelve) activities or experiences that you enjoyed most. This collection of memories will form a more focused picture of you and the manifestations of your true talents. With this picture in mind, you'll be prepared to begin identifying your *Communicational* talents in Exercise Five.

Exercise Five
Discovering Your *Communicational* Talent Strengths

As you reflect on the enjoyed experiences you selected in Exercise Four, use this *Communicational* talent survey to help you identify your *Communicational* strengths. Consider each listed talent as you answer the following question: ***Starting with high school, did your enjoyable life experiences demonstrate an ongoing preference for...***

	No				Yes

1. *Writing words?*   1 2 3 4 5

Communicating thoughts, feelings and ideas clearly in written form, through letters, e-mail, greeting cards, reports, journals, diary entries and research documents. This may be for a variety of purposes—business, journalism, correspondence or personal—and may involve creative expression or rote recording of facts. If you have this talent, you might prefer writing letters to making phone calls.

2. *Conversing?*   1 2 3 4 5

The ability to interact skillfully and enjoyably in conversation, as when talking one-to-one, sharing ideas and feelings, discussing current events, expressing your opinion with one, two or three others (not necessarily using the telephone). You enjoy and excel at interpersonal discussion with mutual give-and-take and understanding.

3. *Giving Speeches or Sermons?*   1 2 3 4 5

Communicating your thoughts and feelings persuasively to a live audience with limited audience discussion; speaking so as to motivate an audience to action. This talent usually favors presenting your opinion to obtain some type of audience response. It does not favor audience give-and-take dialogue (contrast with *Giving Presentation,* talent 15, below). If you're strong in this area, you can gain and hold the audience's attention, increasing their receptiveness to your message. You're a natural speaker; something seems to come alive when you get in front of a group.

No   Yes

4. Teaching?   1 2 3 4 5
Presenting information verbally in a way that enhances understanding, as opposed to presenting your view. Using lecture style to instruct others regarding a subject, normally in a formal classroom setting. Allowing for questions and comments at predetermined breaks, limiting spontaneous audience discussion. As in public speaking (talent 3), this skill involves presenting information clearly (here, to a group or an individual). But while public speaking focuses on emotion, persuasion and application, the teaching talent focuses on deepening understanding and stimulating critical thinking.

5. Broadcasting or Telephone?   1 2 3 4 5
Communicating by electronic media, such as telephone, audio or video recording, radio, television or Internet. The telephone is the most readily available tool, so strength in this area is usually revealed here first. If you possess the broadcasting talent, you enjoy using the phone and electronic media; those without this strength appreciate these tools' convenience but often feel they are too limiting.

6. Designing?   1 2 3 4 5
Expressing thoughts and feelings through graphic media— sketches, illustrations, graphic arts, web design, theater set design, murals, technical illustration and the like.

7. Painting?   1 2 3 4 5
Expressing thoughts and feelings through oils, pastels, watercolors, chalk and similar media. More than a picture; color and texture are part of the communication.

8. Using Colors and Patterns?   1 2 3 4 5
Communicating your thoughts or feelings through the selection of colors and patterns, as in photography, interior décor, choices of clothing, make up, jewelry, house painting, web design, textile design, cake decorating and the like.

9. Using Shapes and Forms?   1 2 3 4 5
The talent for expressing your thoughts or feelings through arranging shapes and forms, as in designing layouts, sculpture, photography (use of light), architectural design, landscaping, furniture arranging and the like. This can involve arrangement of both raw materials and finished objects.

No   Yes
1 2 3 4 5

10. *Using Handcrafts?*

The ability to express your thoughts or feelings through the making of handcrafted items, including wood, plastic, glass, ceramics, leather, fabric, metal, paper and the like. Your skills include, for example, needlepoint, knitting, tile painting and woodcarving. Most people have dabbled in this area, but if you possess it as a strength, you probably enjoy prolonged involvement in it.

11. *Composing or Arranging Music?*

1 2 3 4 5

The ability to express your feelings and thoughts through composing or arranging music. Your artistic skill involves creating or producing music, rather than simply performing it (contrast with talent 14 below).

12. *Acting or Imitating Mannerisms?*

1 2 3 4 5

The talent that excels at projecting a mood or feeling or recreating a character type by changing your external countenance, behavior or personality type. You are able to imitate the mannerisms of others during a conversation, role play, mime or theatrical performances; when telling jokes, as well as when speaking or teaching. Many kindergarten teachers, speakers and politicians have this strength. Surprisingly, this is the key talent for cross-cultural ministry because it enables you to adjust quickly to a new lifestyle and daily habit.

13. *Facilitating Group Discussion?*

1 2 3 4 5

The talent of encouraging an assembled group to share their feelings, opinions, or ideas, as when leading a group study, motivating team members to talk to one another. Many people noted for their instructional ability use moderating as a primary method of communication because they can draw responses out of their students. If this is your strength, you are quick to discern and articulate various positions and how they relate to each other; you make an impartial mediator or debate moderator.

14. *Singing or Instrument Playing?*

1 2 3 4 5

The ability to perform musically, singing or playing an instrument, alone or in front of a group. This involves expression of thoughts or feelings musically, either as part of a group—such as a worship team, choir, orchestra or band—or as a soloist. If you display this talent, you may "become a different person" during your performances. You and others with this talent often amaze others when you get up in front of a church, sing or play, capture the hearts of the congregation, then sit down without saying a word. When engaged in other activities, you may give no clue to the dynamic energy released by your musical performance.

15. *Giving Presentations?*   1 2 3 4 5

The ability to communicate information, to guide a meeting or to elicit a response while in front of an audience. This is the natural talent that enables you to make announcements or lead a meeting or service with give-and-take audience participation—any training, speaking or teaching that involves spontaneous audience interaction. This includes seminar and workshop presentations, leading town hall sessions, serving as Master of Ceremonies, performing product demonstrations, leading management or board briefings. Your performance probably requires no rehearsal.

Review your higher numerical scores above and select one, two or three talents which you feel best describe your *Communicational* strengths. For the largest number of people, *Conversing* will be their preferred choice.

For some, one *Communicational* strength stands alone, with their next best talent only a distant second. Others may have a significant second or third talent, indicating one or two additional strengths.

If selecting your *Communicational* strengths is difficult for you, you can upgrade your assessment to the online IDAK Talent Discovery Guide. Go to *IDAKgroup.com/tdg* for a free preview of the online process.

List your 1-3 *Communicational* strengths below:

1. _____

2. _____

3. _____

Congratulations, You have completed the first of three talent assessment exercises. You'll use these findings later in Exercise Eight (Chapter 6).

Continue to Chapter 4 to learn about your *Relational* talent strength.

Chapter 4
Discovering Your *Relational* Talent Strength

In the world of commerce, everything is based on relationships. You're more likely to buy a car from someone you have built a relationship with than from someone who is a stranger. You're more likely to sign a contract with someone who's proven they care about your success.

Similarly, virtually every ministry involves relationships with one or more people. If the relationships prosper, then the project has a good chance of succeeding. A successful relationship is one in which a trust bond is established, based on the authenticity of those involved. Inauthentic relationships result in shallow friendships and limited success. Authentic relationships create an atmosphere of safety and trust, in which hearts can become open to achieve a shared objective.

In the last chapter we examined the *Communicational* talents. Now we will turn our attention to the second category of natural talents—the three *Relational* talent strengths. Since relationships are so important in ministry, we will explore each of the three *Relational* talents in quite a bit of detail. But before we get into those particulars, let's take a moment aside to address an important question and one of its many answers.

As we've said, a ministry's success rises on the success of relationships. By the same token, we've all seen numerous ministry organizations fall; the primary reason for these failures is…failed relationships. So as we embark on a chapter dealing with *Relational* talents, it makes sense to ask the question, "Why do so many relationships fall short of authenticity and trust?" This is a complex question with many possible answers. We want to briefly address one important factor that either helps or hinders a large number of people in their ability or willingness to establish authentic, trust-based relationships.

It starts with your relationships with your parents, your spouse, your siblings, and your children. God has placed these people in your life, in part, as training opportunities for you to learn how to develop authentic relational bonds with others. Almost everyone enters adulthood with at least one wound or emotional difficulty resulting from one or more of these family relationships. As children, we lacked the maturity and insight to face and resolve these wounds. And so the wounds, if not healed, continue to shape the way we relate to others. But now, as adults, we have the opportunity to make a conscious decision: Will we allow our past responses to our wounds and emotional challenges to determine how we will reach out to others in the future chapters of our lives? Bitterness, unresolved hurt, fear or guilt springing from family relationships will only warp and poison the love we try to convey to others in the gospel message. But healthy recovery from these childhood emotional ailments paves the way for smoothly functioning relationships and a pure presentation of God's compassion and truth.

Will we allow our past to determine our future?

God has provided His love and grace to heal and rebuild—often expressed through friends, the church family and skilled helping professionals. The degree to which one has accepted and applied this spiritual medication will be the degree to which God will trust that person to be His messenger of love and grace to others. God has incredible plans for you, in which you make an eternal impact on others through positive relational connections. If your hurts are hurting your relationships, for the sake of God's kingdom, seek His healing.

Misguided Relational Zeal

God has designed everyone to engage with others in healthy relationships. But not everyone forms relationships in the same way. That's why it's so important to discover the natural *Relational* talent with which God has gifted you. If we misperceive ourselves, we're in danger of pursuing our passion in ways that lead to frustration and disillusionment.

Take Bill, for example. He was attending veterinary school when he responded to a call to commit his life to Jesus Christ. After graduation he started work in a veterinary clinic, and soon also became actively involved in his church, as well as local volunteer ministry opportunities.

Through friends, he learned about a global mission that wanted to start a church in a rural area in Eastern Africa. He became interested in the opportunity and ultimately left his job to join the church-planting team.

Eight years later Bill came to me (John) as a client. The church plant had not succeeded. And it wasn't because he hadn't tried hard enough; he put everything he had into the team effort, including marrying one of the local African women. As I listened to his painful story of disappointments, I marveled at this needless tragedy. It could instead have been a success story, demanding much less effort and bearing much more fruit.

Not everyone forms relationships in the same way.

I asked Bill to complete several aptitude and talent assessment exercises. From the results it was apparent that he was exceptionally gifted with strengths that fit the role of a veterinarian. However, one area he did not appear to excel in was making new friends quickly. And in a foreign country the restrictions of his natural *Relational* style were further compounded by the cross-cultural challenges. Even in his own hometown, Bill needed years to form a trust bond; he encountered only frustration in his attempts to accelerate his natural friendship-developing pace in the African village.

After reviewing the assessments and listening to Bill's still-vital passion for the people in that village, I began to see a different strategy unfolding—a strategy for building the same relationships in the same setting, in a way that better fit with Bill's *Relational* talent. It was quite simple. Yet because it broke from traditional thinking about missions, it had never occurred to Bill.

This was what I proposed: What if Bill were to go to that same village and offer his veterinarian skills to help the famers care for their animals? He would serve as a volunteer, just as he had served in his church-planting role. But with this new approach, villagers would be *seeking him*, asking for his help. They would feel thankful when he cared for and healed their goat, cow, donkey, sheep or chicken. Over three years, Bill's community respect would grow, just because he helped others. The relational flow however, would be reversed. Instead of Bill laboring to try to make friends with the villagers, *the villagers* would be trying to make friends with him, to earn his good will because he had something they wanted—veterinary skill.

The speed with which people form bonds varies considerably.

Then at some future date, after he had gained the trust of the village chief, he could invite a separate church planting team to visit the village. At a village gathering he would introduce the team as his friends and ask the villagers to listen to what his friends had to say. I think the villagers would be more inclined to listen, since Bill had earned their trust and respect by listening and meeting their immediate needs first. And he would have enjoyed doing it in a way that was natural for him.

The end result? Bill felt affirmed for who he was. He learned that he is gifted perfectly to make a contribution. He had simply been trying to force an introvert-shaped peg into an extrovert-shaped hole.

Bill's example illustrates the fact that God has gifted all men and women with natural talents for developing relationships. Yes, *all* types of people—no exceptions—have the God-given capacity to form trust bonds with others. Yet our study of thousands of assessments have shown that the *speed* with which people form bonds varies considerably. Speed of relationship development is the main distinction between the three *Relational* talents.

So what are these *Relational* talents that we humans possess? Let's begin at the gregarious end of the spectrum with...

The *Multi-Relational* Talent

Some people form sincere trust bonds with new acquaintances in minutes or hours. They're called *Multi-Relational*. It makes their day to develop a new, genuine friendship at a wedding reception, with the hotel housekeeper, or with the head cook at a retreat center. Most of us stand in awe of these people's graceful manner. We've tried to imitate them, and for many of us our efforts have resulted in stress and pent-up anxiety. They have a natural talent for quick relationship building.

Approximately 15 percent of the population has this unique gift. In other words, God has gifted about 15 percent of humanity to meet and befriend new acquaintances very quickly with a sincere trust bond—a process that even gives some of them an adrenalin rush.

The *Singular Relational* Talent

At the extreme opposite pole is the person who takes years to form a trust bond—this person we call *Singular Relational*. God in His wisdom, for His purpose, has gifted some with the capacity for developing trust bonds slowly, gradually. As these trust bonds grow and strengthen, they tend to last longer and go deeper than bonds that the *Multi-Relational* develops. For people with either trait, relationships achieve an authentic trust bond level, yet one gets there faster than the other. Throughout the *Singular Relational's* longer process, however, he or she continues to make the relationship a priority and cultivates much greater depths of transparency and authenticity. Research shows that God has gifted about 15 percent of us as *Singular Relational*.

Now, lest you devalue this *Relational* talent, let's pause for a moment to consider: If you were to select someone from one of these two extremes as your spiritual mentor, which stereotype would you choose? Most would choose the *Singular Relational*, because once you've achieved a trust bond with that person, you'll become one of their top five relational priorities for years to come. This was Bill's *Relational* strength.

The point is that people along the full spectrum of *Relational* talents are equally important to God's kingdom plans. Accept your innate *Relational* strength with gratitude. God doesn't want any of us to stress out, trying to be someone we are not.

The *Familiar Group Relational* Talent

We've examined the two extremes. Is there a *Relational* talent somewhere in the middle? Most certainly, yes. And this talent belongs to approximately 70 percent of us. It's called *Familiar Group Relational*. The person with this in-the-middle relational capacity tends to build trust bonds over a period of nine to twelve months. So to be at the top of his or her relational game, this person takes about a year to form genuine relationships. That is why door-to-door evangelism only works for a few (the *Multi-Relationals*), while home Bible study groups work for most of us.

Now that we've briefly touched on all three *Relational* talents, how does identifying yours help you find your future ideal ministry role? Consider the job duties of a media technician for a video production ministry. This saint spends hours shooting and editing film, which may involve dealing with new people to a small extent, but doesn't require a *Multi-Relational* talent to love and serve people. On the other hand, a church planter, who must deal with new faces almost every day, will be more successful with *Multi-* or *Familiar Group* natural abilities. You can begin to see that your *Relational* talent is a huge factor to consider in predicting a best fit for your future calling.

Censoring the Extrovert

To further illustrate the importance of discovering your *Relational* talent strength, let's take a look at a story that's a virtual photonegative of Bill's story, above. Chet was a pastor who faithfully served his denomination for over twenty years in a rural area of the Eastern US. Actually, Chet had served in several rural churches over those two decades. Finally, his denominational district requested my (John's) assistance, reporting that Chet's performance had been marginal. They wanted to evaluate his future capacity for pastoral leadership.

Chet completed several tests and exercises, along with an interview assessment which I perform to evaluate natural talents. I was surprised to find that Chet appeared to possess the *Multi-Relational* strength. Normally this strength would be a significant asset to any pastor, providing a major boost in winning over the trust and confidence of congregation members. However, in this situation Chet's outgoing nature came under suspicion within the more insular, narrow-minded rural communities. When Chet recruited new community visitors to join the church, rather than welcoming them, the established congregants viewed these visitors as outsiders upsetting the integrity of the congregational family.

My experience has been that too many rural churches are comprised almost exclusively of members whose lineage goes back to the founding great great grandparents, who lived during the Civil War, or even earlier. Any newcomer would need to endure a long probationary period, proving his or her longevity before being considered part of the family. Few, if any, *Multi-Relationals* would be able to last long in that type of cloistered fellowship. Most *Multi-Relationals* are attracted to large churches where they can continually meet new people.

All are wired by God to be able to build honest relationships.

So time after time Chet, blessed with the ability and desire to make new friends quickly, found himself limited to friendships within the hundred or fewer members in each rural church. Chet didn't understand the dynamic that placed limits on his ability to bond with new visitors, and in a short time he would typically become frustrated and want to move on to new relational territory.

When Chet's talent assessment revealed the simple fact that he was gifted by God with the *Multi-Relational* talent, his entire countenance changed. He was suddenly freed to expand his ministry vision so that he could look for opportunities that were more people-intensive. Now he could serve God according to his strengths, rather than force himself into an inappropriate mold.

Bonding for Every *Relational* Strength

People of all *Relational* talents and all personality types—all are wired by God to be able to build honest relationships. Some people will take long years to make a few good friends, and some will make a dozen genuine friends in a single day. The common theme in all authentic relationships is a foundation of trust, based on proven character. Jesus is our model: "who committed no sin, nor was deceit found in His mouth" (1 Peter 2:22). If you build each relationship by demonstrating integrity, the other person will likely want to be truthful and vulnerable with you.

Even if you're a *Multi-Relational*, you must understand that honest relationships take time to build. They begin with your expressing interest in the other person's family, job, hobbies and needs—demonstrating to a skeptical, skittish, wounded heart that you care. This is true in Nigeria, in North Chicago and in your neighborhood. And as we've assisted people who are preparing for ministry, we've discovered that before going anywhere to touch lives, if one can't do relationships right in his own community, he can't expect to do them well in another culture.

Trying to force the getting-to-know-you process feels plastic and can cause the other person to back away. In a ministry context, a new acquaintance is not likely to be persuaded to become bosom buddies with you or your friend Jesus in three minutes with a booklet. Regardless of how we are gifted relationally, all of us need to be intentional and patient about demonstrating integrity, honesty and genuine compassion in order to develop healthy God-honoring relationships. But if we take the time and make the effort, any of us can bond closely with others.

I (Nelson) saw this illustrated when I went with a group on a two-week ministry trip to a family camp in Russia. Our ministry team was permitted to provide activities for children of all ages and conduct topical workshops for adults. As you would expect, one of the team goals was to establish good relationships, and thereby to earn the right to share joy, life and the content of the gospel. We observed that with grade school kids it was possible to earn their trust and the right to share Christ in just a few days. With junior-high-age kids, the time required was more like the entire two weeks. And when the participants tried to establish trust with high-school-age young people, the two-week stint in the country wasn't enough. To build a from-scratch relationship with an adult in this cross-cultural situation would have taken much longer. Generally, the older people get, the stronger the wall of skepticism they tend to build, and consequently they are to slower to trust.

To earn the right to be heard and used in the lives of people, *you must give your time.* When you do, others will gradually come to see and trust your heart. Relational trust is spelled T–I–M–E.

Exercise Six
Discovering Your *Relational* Talent Strength

Let's return to our talent assessment survey. Do you recall the ten or so most enjoyed experiences you identified in Exercise Four (Chapter 3)? Think of the overall picture that these activities portray. What is the "people environment" in this picture? Is it a large and ever-changing sea of faces, or is it spending time by yourself or perhaps with a trusted friend? What is your preferred relational setting, where you feel the most relaxed and energized?

Starting with high school, did your enjoyable life experiences demonstrate an ongoing preference for relating to people as a...

	No	Yes
	1 2 3 4 5	

16. *Multi-Relational?*
Quickly bonding with new acquaintances. You make new friends easily upon first encounter, even getting a "rush" from forming new friendships. You're probably capable of maintaining multiple relationships over an extended period of time, comfortable around new people as well as people you already know.

17. *Familiar Group Relational?*   1 2 3 4 5
Bonding with others over a nine- to twelve-month period, preferring to be with people you already know, seeking to continuously deepen existing relationships. You establish rapport with people after repeated meetings, and you enjoy joint work projects, department meetings or group sessions. You're probably capable of strengthening and sustaining group membership, and you're relationally flexible—willing to meet new people or work on a task by yourself.

18. *Singular Relational?*   1 2 3 4 5
Preferring to be by yourself, engaging in work or leisure activities that do not require starting or maintaining relationships—such as reading, studying, solitaire, woodworking, gardening, interior decorating, auto repair and

the like. You establish rapport with people after long-term contact, and you may be willing to hang out or work long-term with one or two people you have come to know well.

Review your higher numerical scores above and select the one *Relational* talent which most consistently describes the way you form friendship and trust bonds. Most people will have more than one *Relational* talent with high "Yes" scores. If you do, then write *"Familiar Group"* as your one best *Relational* talent, because this talent is flexible and is likely to include certain aspects of the other two.
If this is a difficult selection for you to make, you may want to supplement this survey with the more in-depth online Talent Discovery Guide at *IDAKgroup.com/tdg*.

List your one preferred *Relational* talent below:

_____

Good job. You've now completed the second of three talent assessment exercises. You'll use this result later in Exercise Eight (Chapter 6).
    Next is Chapter 5, concerning your *Functional* talent strengths.

Chapter 5
Discovering Your *Functional* Talent Strengths

Tom came to me (John) frustrated and despondent. He had retired from a high-level position doing research for an engineering-related company. Tom had a doctorate in mechanical engineering and felt God's prompting to get involved in overseas ministry work. He had completed several short-term team mission projects and was active in his church's mission program, but no sending agency would consider him because they didn't have a place for a mechanical engineer with a doctorate.

When Tom and I looked at his talent profile, one natural talent strength stood out—*Researching and Investigating* (Talent 47). Tom had a knack for searching out information and would use his skill for everyday pursuits, like finding the best buy on a refrigerator or selecting the most productive financial stocks to purchase. Unfortunately, both Tom and the mission agencies viewed this natural asset as an engineering ability that did not apply to evangelism, discipleship or church planting overseas.

I recall sharing Tom's story with about fifty mission representatives at a conference, emphasizing his natural ability for *Researching*. I was also careful not to mention his previous education or career. Several hands shot up and one mission recruiter said, "Hey, we really need a skilled researcher." I later shared that story with Tom and helped him get in touch with those who had expressed interest in him.

Both Tom and the ministry recruiters had made the same mistake. They'd interpreted Tom's past occupation as part of this essential identity, when in reality *we are not what we have done.* They just could not look beyond Tom's job title and educational background. It was only when Tom realized that he had a transferrable and much-needed talent (among several others) that things began to connect.

We are not what we have done.

Communicating with ministry organizations about your natural talents—not just your past occupations and accomplishments—will give you a stronger, more flexible opportunity to explore future options. This is especially true if you believe you've spent fifteen or twenty years in a job that does not represent the real you. You may feel like you're just putting in your time. Your current career is draining you, burning you out instead of energizing you. You wish you could wake up eager to meet the day. You long to serve in a way that will finally put into practice the strengths God has given you.

Discovering your *Functional* or task-oriented talents completes the full circle of your talent strengths. Your *Communicational, Relational* and *Functional* talents will help you identify the types of job duties that will fit you best, will bring you greatest fulfillment and will maximize your eternal kingdom impact—whether the new job is exactly like your old one, nothing like it, or somewhere in the middle.

Games *Functional* Talents Play

We've been working through three talent classifications. We've seen the *Communicational* and *Relational* talents. The last, and largest, category includes the thirty-six *Functional* talents, which are clustered into thirteen subgroups (take a glance at Exercise Seven at the end of this chapter for a quick overview of these subgroups). The *Functional* talent category represents your more concrete, task-oriented aptitudes—specific traits that will help you define your ideal ministry job duties. Here and there throughout this chapter we will highlight various *Functional* talents and talent subgroups—those that are particularly important to understand, or those that are often misunderstood—sometimes explaining how the talents differ from and interact with each other.

Let's start right out with one talent that relates to your personal organizational skills—*Ordering Your Space* (*Functional* Talent 20). You may have a strength for *Ordering Your Space* if you're compulsive about keeping things in their proper place. Maybe you like to maintain order in policies and procedures, keeping things the way they are supposed to be. A few of us are obsessive about this organizational trait. And even many who aren't gifted at organization have learned to be adequate in this area because ordering work space can directly relate to job productivity.

In contrast, another segment of us are obsessively repelled by organizing things. They wage a daily battle against the everything-in-its-place expectation. With many exceptions, these tend to be creative types, such as musicians, artists and designers. Such as both of us, your authors. Our experience with thousands of assessments has shown that those of us who tend to be idea people, prone to experimenting and tinkering—those whose gifts belong to the subgroup including *Being Creative, Imagining* and *Inventing* (*Functional* Talents 21–23)—are not as naturally orderly as our brothers and sisters. We are not as inclined to favor tradition, structure and policies. We always question everything, we think outside the box. We change recipes, woodworking patterns and long-accepted work procedures. At heart, until something stands the test of being questioned to death, we consider continuous improvement (change) the rule. A *Creative* person might say to an *Ordering Your Space* person, "Focus on doing the right thing rather than doing the thing right."

> *We see the world and its problems differently.*

So, naturally, clashes frequently arise between the keepers of tradition and the iconoclasts who continually seek to improve or change tradition. Such conflicts reside at the heart of many church splits, management disagreements, board disputes and even educational policy disagreements.

God has gifted each of us differently. So we see the world and its problems differently and we seek to address them in different ways. Which approach is right? The answer is both/and. We need the consistency of tradition and order along with the continuous questioning and experimenting to find a better way. When both approaches are valued and work together, everyone wins. So both approaches need to be represented in important decisions, on boards and management teams.

In the pages that follow, we're going to encounter a few more examples where certain talents tend to clash. Just as with the healthy, cooperative relationship we've just described between *Creative* and *Ordering Your Space* talents, so we also urge attitudes of mutual respect, balance and harmony between any other pairings of talents that tend toward conflict.

Misguided *Functional* Zeal

One subgroup of *Functional* talents to highlight has to do with the ways God has gifted us to oversee, supervise or manage the strengths of others as we all attempt to do His will. God has gifted some at *Initiating and Developing* (Talent 24). These are entrepreneurs and visionaries who see needs and opportunities. They can mobilize individuals to seize the initiative and plant a church or begin an outreach ministry to the inner city neighborhoods. Entrepreneurs have this talent strength, for example. God has gifted others with a natural talent for *Long-Range Planning* (Talent 25)—foreseeing the sequential scheduling details that involve people, money, time and equipment. They can intuitively figure out how long a project or goal will take, how much it will cost and how many people will be needed. God has gifted still others to fit the traditional general *Managing* role (Talent 26). They provide stability for an organization, helping each of us maximize our strengths individually while working as part of a team.

We urge attitudes of mutual respect, balance and harmony.

Our observation and research have shown that these talents appear to be polarized. This means that no one person will have more than one of these strenths, if any. And people gifted with different of these strengths will have different intuitive approaches to leading an organization.

All of these supervisory talents are important, but they involve very different approaches to running a church, a company or a ministry organization. These differences can lead to heated disputes, even among men and women who are seasoned and experienced leaders.

A related but different problem arose for Sally, some time after she had been hired for a new position to assist the president of a company. Sally previously had been the co-owner of a business with her husband, which they sold. She was experienced and understood the discretion needed when handling delicate matters. The new president asked me (John) to evaluate Sally's talent strengths so that he could be sure that her new job description fit her aptitudes.

Sally's talent profile showed several key strengths that would be very useful to assist the president, including *Ordering Time and Priorities* (Talent 19). This meant that she would be very efficient with her time and get projects completed on schedule. Yet, there was one additional talent she appeared to possess which on the surface seemed to be an asset for this position. This talent was *Long-Range Planning* (Talent 25). The president liked this because his natural gift was *Initiating and Developing* (Talent 24); he would "shoot from the hip" with new ideas and programs. He correctly reasoned that Sally could help him map things out so that he would be less impulsive and think things through before taking action. However, what the president did not realize was that the *Long-Range Planning* talent brought with it a need to be in charge of the planning process so that the intuitive planning process can be completed appropriately. Sally, as a new employee, did not understand how significantly her job duties would limit her—that she was not to be in charge, but only to give advice when asked.

The conflict had come to a head when the president called me about a year later, facing a dilemma. He was very happy with Sally's job performance, but he was also complaining that she was spending too much time planning out her own projects, which he had given her, and did not contribute equal time to assist with his projects. Fortunately, the story ended happily. The president appreciated Sally's strength in *Planning* and rewrote her job description to allow her more autonomous responsibility.

> *Sally had key strengths that would be useful to assist the president.*

Everyone won out on the arrangement, the president gained a much more productive employee (now a department head), Sally was more highly motivated, and the company benefitted when Sally's wise input brought balance to the president's entrepreneurial ventures.

The Case of the Hindered Helpers

One more subgroup is the *Helping Others* talents (*Functional Talents 31–34*). These aptitudes are the soothing ointment that God has provided for the body, bringing nurture and healing to those who hurt. These gifted individuals will readily clear their busy schedule for someone in crisis. They can patiently listen and remain compassionately close by while we cry out in pain and suffering.

Frank and Sharon personified the *Helping* talents, but when they were referred to me (John), they came with a boatload of frustration. They had been exploring future ministry options overseas, but numerous organizations had turned them down. When we reviewed their talent profiles, we discovered that they had a combination of *Helping* talent strengths—namely, *Being of Service* and *Reassuring and Supporting* (Talents 32 and 34). These fit well with the job duties of providing hospitality, among other ministry roles. They also shared a passion for the military and for European countries. It was not rocket science to suggest that they look into providing a hospitality ministry to servicemen and women who were stationed overseas, a home away from home. Frank and Sharon indicated that they too had come to this conclusion, but were not successful in applying for that type of position.

The Helping talents are the soothing ointment God has provided for the body.

At this point our conversation changed from trying to find a good fit to communicating one's strengths with the right ministry team. What Frank and Sharon had failed to do was to explain in their agency application and interview process that their true identity—how God had gifted them—included these very potent *Helping* talents. Unfortunately, both of their previous jobs were in no way related to hospitality, and they had been repeatedly screened out on the first pass. I encouraged them to get beyond the filling out of forms and talk directly to a staff person for each of the agencies that fit their passion for serving overseas servicemen and women. I don't know what happened after my service with Frank and Sharon concluded, but I do know they were much relieved that they had a future in what God had gifted them to do.

The *Helping* talents are certainly applicable to ministry service, but they often clash with the *Supervisory* talents (Talents 24–26) in terms of decision making. The *Helping* talents tend to focus on individual needs and hurts as the criteria for making policy decisions, while the *Supervisory* talents focus more on the big picture—what is good for the team, the organization, or the comprehensive cause. If your talent strengths lie in either of these subgroups, be aware of this potential conflict, and be prepared to work toward mutual respect for one another's values and gifts.

Three Misunderstood Talents

Although *Being Physically Active* (Talent 27) is the proverbial "athletic" talent, many who have it are not accomplished athletes. People with this talent have total body motor coordination. In plain English this means that one's body wants to be in constant motion. Many who are of an athletic bent express this talent through daily exercise—jogging, racquetball, the gym, swimming and so forth. But whether sports-oriented or not, those who possess this talent should not aspire to a desk-type ministry position, confined to a small workspace on the tenth floor. They need work that requires continuous or frequent movement—in and out of the car, up and down the stairs, back and forth to meetings... You get the idea.

The Solving Problems talent seeks out the root cause of an issue.

Solving Problems (Talent 46) is a popular talent—many people want it. But not everyone who wants it, has it. Take careful note of your behavior patterns as you discern whether or not this is one of your strengths. This talent is continually seeking to go below the surface in figuring out the root cause of an issue or malfunction. In relationships, the compulsion is to continually try to figure out what makes Julian tick—why he does not get along with his wife, why he is so quiet and withdrawn, why he avoids church socials, and so on. Not for the sake of knowledge in itself, but in order to diagnose and resolve the problem. True problem solvers ask questions like: *Why is this grocery line so long (and what would make it move faster)? What is causing the fluctuation in the housing market (and how can I get an edge)?* Unfortunately, these people can also have a critical spirit and be prone to prying into problems that are none of their business.

Many with the Analyzing talent end up in higher education.

This talent tends to clash with the *Multi-Relational* talent (*Relational* Talent 16). The *Solving Problems* talent wants to size up a new acquaintance before deciding to befriend him or her. In contrast, a *Multi-Relational* rarely will size up a person to determine qualification for befriending them, and they may become offended if the other person is slow to reciprocate. The *Solving Problems* talent also likes continuous education, as long as it is practical and will apply to one's job duties.

Analyzing (Talent 50) is a distant cousin to *Solving Problems* (Talent 46), but is quite distinct. This talent seeks to go under the surface regarding a topic *just to better understand*, without any interest in applying that learning. *Solving Problems*, on the other hand, wants to understand in order to improve. Many with the *Analyzing* talent end up occupationally in higher education, where a person is paid to learn. This talent may not be friendly to business or practical, hands-on ministry service—both of which want to get to practical application, not just information.

A Bible teacher with the *Analyzing* talent can delight in digging into Scripture for the sheer joy of learning, rather than the more practical goal of equipping others with guidelines for living. If you possess this talent as a strength, God put it there for a specific reason. You should seek a position that allows time for you to continually learn, but with an outlet, through which your learning can be shared with other hungry learners.

Is It Worth the Risk to Serve God's Way?

In a moment you'll begin Exercise Seven, which will help you discover your *Functional* talents. This may simply reinforce what you already knew about yourself. Or it might reveal something new about your God-given strengths—something that you didn't know about yourself. Maybe something that feels threatening, because it means God might be calling you do perform a type of task you never considered, or never thought you could do. God may be using this book to open the door to a new adventure for you. Perhaps you feel the adrenaline beginning to pump—from anticipation (if you like novelty and the unknown), or from apprehension (if you don't think of yourself as "the adventuresome type").

I (John) recall interviewing a speech pathologist named Andrea who was burned out with all of the paperwork in her job. She wanted to find something more enjoyable, with less stress. As I listened further to her life story, I noted that many of her statements reflected a lack of confidence. Andrea recalled that during her time in school she did not like to raise her hand in class. When serving in a "soup kitchen" for the homeless, she preferred to be in the back washing the dishes rather than up front serving the food. Given her timidity, she had long ago concluded that she had no significant strengths to offer in a ministry organization.

God may be using this book to open the door to a new adventure.

I knew that Andrea's self-perception was based on a misperception, but convincing her that God had gifted her for a special place of service would require her to take what might feel like two huge risks. She would first have to risk abandoning her comfortable self-deprecation by accepting that she possessed certain specific talents as gifts from God. She would then have to risk the unknown by making a commitment to something she had never done before, actively developing those traits and moving out to reach others. Even though she was exceptionally gifted in *Reassuring and Supporting* (*Functional* Talent 34, below) and *Being of Service* (*Functional* Talent 32), she wouldn't fulfill her potential until she internalized the evidence and took a stand regarding her importance to God's plan.

Most of Andrea's life had been a sad process of avoidance, even when she was performing in her strengths. But to her credit (and by God's healing love and grace), she gradually took ownership of God's view of her, making it her self-concept. With this came a sense of worth and a growing confidence that she did indeed possess significant strengths that could be used fruitfully in ministry.

You can possess all kinds of abilities and knowledge. But if you don't take the risk of moving out confidently and using the talents God has given you, you may experience only disappointment and underachievement in spite of your considerable God-given natural talents. It comes down to a question of your will, your choice—to consciously trust God and take a risk on employing, investing and expending all of your resources, including your talents. You may worry and fret. *What will the results say about me? Will they confirm my fears?* But God answers, *It's not about you. Here's the real question: What will your all-out, enthusiastic service say about Me as I work through you?*

God asks, What will your service say about Me as I work through you?

The apostle Paul took on the goal of spreading the gospel throughout the then-known world in his lifetime. His traveling companion Luke had the same passion for God, but fulfilled it in a different way. God wants people with that kind of no-holds-barred willingness, that kind of passion. Paul and Luke risked everything, never taking his eye off the goal. He was by no means fully confident in his direction at every decision point; he wrestled with uncertainty and doubt. Often Paul would ask his friends to pray for him for boldness. Yet Paul is one of the most courageous characters in the Bible.

Acts 19:23–41 tells the story of the time Paul stirred the city of Ephesus, which resulted in a riotous mob within the city arena. Paul's friends urged him to stay away. Instead, he wanted to go *into* the arena to speak the truth for God. Our mission is to become key components of organizations that go eagerly into neighborhoods and nations; to be part of God's plan to disciple the nations, whether across town or across the ocean.

Your abilities and your will power are not your source of victory—God is. "For it is God who works in you both to will and to do for His good pleasure" (Philippians 2:13). So trust Him, because "without faith it is impossible to please Him" (Hebrews 11:6). Unfortunately the term "faith" has lost its full impact in our day. Think of it this way: We place our faith in cars and airplanes to get us safely to our destinations. We risk our lives in those vehicles. So we understand better the writer's meaning if we hear him exhorting us with the paraphrase: "Without risking something for God, it's impossible to please Him."

The same author voiced a boomer-type attitude when we wrote: "Therefore strengthen the hands which hang down, and the feeble knees, and make straight paths for your feet" (Hebrews 12:12–13). Our culture might put the attitude in these words: Just do it! The writer wanted to change the world for Christ. This is not to say that you need to risk your physical life or run into harm's way. It is also not to say that you need to be the point person on the front lines (although this might be the case for individuals with the appropriate gifting). Nor is this to advocate blind leaps into the unknown; in fact, in Chapter 8 you will learn to "test the water" of an opportunity before you dive in.

Rather, we are saying that in order to maximize God's love through you, you may need to risk joining a team of other servants when you'd prefer to go it alone. You may need to put your plans and reputation on the altar to get fully involved in God's calling for you. And you may need to risk accepting a ministry job that uses talents you never realized could be used for God. Those talents could end up shaping your identity into something different from what it was in your former work life. That change might seem frightening on the front side, but the reward is worth the risk. You'll look back with a sigh of relief and gratitude. Without your steps of faith, you might have missed a valuable opportunity.

You can do it, because you're called by a great and good God. He promises to work in you and through you to accomplish greater things. He will use you to extend His kingdom, if given the chance. Be willing to think outside the box of human perspective. Ask the God of miracles to express his love through you in ways that can only be by His enabling power.

"If you ever encounter a theology that doesn't directly connect the greatness of God with your potential to go great things on His behalf, it's not biblical theology. File it under heresy."
—Steven Furtick in *Sun Stand Still*

Exercise Seven
Discovering Your *Functional* Talent Strengths

Recall your ten enjoyable experiences, which you selected in Exercise Four (Chapter 3). As you think on these, consider what types of consistent task-oriented behavior you appeared to favor. Use the talent survey to help you select 3–5 strengths.

Starting with high school, did your most enjoyable life experiences demonstrate an ongoing preference for...

Organizing Personal Time and Space

These talents involve the effective and efficient use of one's time and space. You may have one, both or neither of these talents as strengths.

                                                        No   Yes

19. *Ordering Time and Priorities?*   1 2 3 4 5

Organizing your personal time to maximize efficiency, multitasking, preparing to-do lists or schedules, trying to squeeze the most out of each hour or day. Enables one to set priorities, evaluate timing and recognize efficiency. This talent deals with scheduling personal time and differs from *Long-Range Planning* (talent 25, below), which schedules time for others.

20. *Ordering Your Space?*   1 2 3 4 5

Routinely putting things back where they belong, keeping your surroundings well organized—your closet, desk, work space, automobile—keeping household items in their place, maintaining the order of established standards, policies and programs. Obviously, people with this talent are "neat." But not all neat people have this talent. Some keep the appearance of neatness but are not well organized, such as the person who clears off the top of the dresser by shoving everything into a drawer.

Being Creative

This group of abilities describes the formation of new associations with previously unrelated concepts, objects or thoughts. You may have one, two, three or none of these talents as strengths.

	No	Yes

21. *Being Creative?*   1 2 3 4 5

Originating new and different ways to do things, improving routine tasks, looking at traditions with a new perspective, pursuing continuous improvement, questioning outdated regulations or policies, thinking outside the box. Forming new ideas for systems, concepts or methods.

22. *Imagining?*   1 2 3 4 5

Originating ideas for stories, theories or other abstract concepts. Spending time fantasizing new story adventures, imagining new science fiction ideas, originating a real life drama with characters, conceptualizing philosophical perspectives.

23. *Inventing?*   1 2 3 4 5

Originating new gadgets, formulas, prototypes, machines, hybrids and the like—whether mechanical, electrical, electronic, chemical or other physical devices. This talent likes to create tools or methods around the house to simplify chores or improve hobby procedures.

Supervising Others

This group includes talents in directing the behavior and activities of others. You may have one, two, three or none of these talents as strengths.

24. *Initiating and Developing?*   1 2 3 4 5

Envisioning and leading new startup programs, projects or ventures, recruiting others to the launch phase and coordinating their initial activities—including new products, departments, clubs, organizations, companies, partnerships and the like. This is the talent for being a the entrepreneur. It is also called the change agent or "turnaround" talent.

	No	Yes
	1 2 3	4 5

25. *Long-Range Planning?*

Mapping out the long-range details to meet organizational goals for a company, church, club, family, financial venture. Considers time, costs, equipment, personnel and facilities. Enjoys developing all the details for a long family vacation— travel, lodging, meals, expenses, what to wear and so on. Includes scheduling the activities of others to reach goals.

26. *Managing?*

1 2 3 4 5

Overseeing others in an established organization, company, club, department or church with the expectation to bring out the best in each team member. Supervising and coordinating an established group to build unity and team cooperation toward a common goal. This talent is the main stabilizing factor in most organizations.

Using Body, Hands or Fingers

This group of talents describes four different types of body-motor coordination. You may have one, two, three, four or none of these talents as strengths.

27. *Being Physically Active?*

1 2 3 4 5

Using your body, arms and legs in a coordinated way, as in athletics, dancing, physical labor, exercising, construction work, gardening and the like.

28. *Using Hands and Arms?*

1 2 3 4 5

Physical agility in tasks using hand and arm, such as using hand tools or power tools, repairing (a car, furniture, clothes, equipment, a fence), building or assembling (cabinets, equipment, landscaping), adjusting and the like. It is a necessary talent for mechanics, carpenters and plumbers.

29. *Operating and Driving?*

1 2 3 4 5

This is the talent for operating a moving vehicle, heavy equipment, or stationary machines—a car, truck, aircraft, boat, forklift, tractor, construction and landscape equipment or industrial and factory equipment.

No   Yes
1 2 3 4 5

30. *Using Hands and Fingers?*
Manual dexterity in precision detail projects, such as building small-scale model kits, soldering, jewelry making, calligraphy, drafting, needlepoint, sewing and the like. This is an important talent for dentists, surgeons, watchmakers, jewelry makers and those who build and repair computers and other electronic devices.

Helping Others
This group of talents can be described as a natural availability to come alongside to meet the needs of others. People with these talents usually focus more on others' needs rather than one's own personal priorities. You may have one, two, three, four or none of these talents as strengths.

31. *Tutoring?*
1 2 3 4 5

Helping another to cope with disabilities or learning problems. Providing special training, coaching, nurturing, academic tutoring, therapy or rehabilitation one-to-one over an extended period of time. This is not necessarily a classroom teaching talent. Parents who have nurtured a disabled child, special education teachers, social workers and others who help the disadvantaged may have this talent.

32. *Being of Service?*
1 2 3 4 5

Assisting others by being available when they need help with their projects and programs, sometimes helping to the neglect of your projects and time schedule.

33. *Counseling?*
1 2 3 4 5

Patiently helping people over an extended period of time to resolve personal or emotional issues, such as dating, marriage, self-image, conflicts, spiritual concerns, abnormal behavior and the like. Focusing on the emotional needs or problems of others and then helping them with suggestions, advice or direction.

34. *Reassuring and Supporting?*
1 2 3 4 5

Identifying with another's hurts, frustrations and anxieties; encouraging, nurturing, comforting, supporting without necessarily trying to solve another's problems.

Using Intuition

This is the ability to evaluate one's surroundings without the conscious use of reasoning. No one's intuition is right all the time, but those with talents in this category are right often enough to rely upon their "senses." You may have one, two or none of these talents as strengths.

	No Yes
	1 2 3 4 5

35. *Evaluating Character?*   1 2 3 4 5
The ability to quickly and accurately assess another's integrity or sincerity, including motives, underlying thoughts or attitude. Those who are intuitive about "reading" the behavior of animals (such as dogs and horses) are normally gifted with the ability to "read" people's motives as well.

36. *Making Future Projections?*   1 2 3 4 5
The ability to accurately predict the public's responses to future events, as in politics, clothing fads, business trends, international confrontations or other future concerns. Forecasting (foreseeing) future developments in personal or public circles, including public opinion.

Being Persuasive

These talents enable one to direct others to a course of action, a change of mood or a commitment to follow. You may have one, two, three or none of these talents as strengths.

37. *Negotiating?*   1 2 3 4 5
Successfully settling disputes between two or more parties, acting as a go-between, arbitrating, negotiating contracts, being a peacemaker and the like.

38. *Selling?*   1 2 3 4 5
Successfully convincing someone to pay for a product or service. Recruiting volunteers, fund raising, closing the sale. Traditionally, salespeople have been characterized negatively, but there is a legitimate place for honest sellers in ministry service—they make wonderful recruiters and fund raisers.

No   Yes
1 2 3 4 5

39. *Promoting?*
*Motivating others to consider something that you are
excited about*—a new book, new restaurant, sale item, new
viewpoint, spiritual perspective, political candidate and the
like.

Observing Details
These talents involve visual attention to fine points. You may
have one, two, three or none of these talents as strengths.

40. *Observing Physical Environment?*   1 2 3 4 5
Seeing details that others often miss, outdoors or indoors—
such as identifying a bird specie, type of small flower or
animal track. Noticing small rock formations, rust, scratches,
cracks, carpet stains and the like. Finding a garment flaw,
paint scratch, or missing part before making a purchase.

41. *Observing Text Details?*   1 2 3 4 5
*Seeing details that others often miss in written or printed
matter*—websites, news print, magazines, contracts,
manuscripts, reports, blueprints, maps—including
misspellings, typos, grammatical errors, or drawing errors.
Proofreaders need to notice printed details. Machinists often
need to see blueprint details.

42. *Observing in 3D?*   1 2 3 4 5
*The ability to visualize a three-dimensional object from a
two-dimensional drawing,* such as a finished building from
a blueprint, a completed cabinet from a sketch, a finished
garment from a pattern.

Using Numbers
These enable one to use figures readily and accurately. You
may have one, two or none of these as strengths.

43. *Calculating Numbers?*   1 2 3 4 5
Mentally working quickly and accurately with numbers and
figures. Adding, subtracting, multiplying and dividing without
much effort.

	No	Yes

44. *Recording and Auditing?*   No 1 2 3 4 5 Yes

Routinely counting and recording how many items are on a shelf, in a box, in a room in a warehouse. Taking inventory. Keeping track of mileage, expenses, items used, weight, nutritional intake. Keeping track of household items which need to be replenished for the next shopping trip.

Problem Solving Procedures
The ability to discover the source of failure, breakdown or error. You may have one, two or none of these talents as strengths.

45. *Technical Troubleshooting?*   1 2 3 4 5

Tinkering with and diagnosing problems in mechanical, electrical, electronic, chemical or other technical items. Taking apart and repairing clocks, bicycle gears, lawnmower engines, auto engines, circuit boards, door locks, computers, appliances and the like.

46. *Solving Problems?*   1 2 3 4 5

Continuously thinking deeply about how to resolve concerns such as people conflicts, political issues, international issues, contract misunderstandings, family relations, employee relations, church member relations, leadership clashes and the like. The ability to diagnose errors in human logic, administrative procedures or interpersonal relationships.

Note: Don't confuse *Technical Troubleshooting* or *Solving Problems* with *Analyzing* (talent 50, below), which is one of the talents in the Reasoning and Contemplating category. An *Analyzing* talent searches for knowledge about why things (positively) *are* the way they are—what makes things "tick." In contrast, the *Technical Troubleshooting* or *Solving Problems* talents assess why something is (negatively) *not* the way it's supposed to be, trying to get to the root cause of a problem that needs solving, and then fixing it.

Handling Information

The ability to deal with facts, data and other types of raw information. You may have one, two, three or none of these talents as strengths.

No   Yes

47. *Researching and Investigating?*   1 2 3 4 5
Collecting information from multiple sources about a subject, a proposed purchase, a future venture, an investment, a future vacation destination, a proposed restaurant, a book to read and the like.

48. *Remembering?*   1 2 3 4 5
Easily and quickly recalling detailed information—names, dates, numbers, addresses, events, qualities and the like.

49. *Classifying?*   1 2 3 4 5
Routinely, efficiently arranging and maintaining information for quick, easy reference—such as reports, photographs, recipes and the like—perhaps using a computer filing system, desk filing system or catalogue system.

Reasoning and Contemplating

These talents focus on the mental processing of information. You may have one, two, three or none of these talents as strengths.

50. *Analyzing?*   1 2 3 4 5
Continuously seeking to understand most any object, idea or system. Curiously studying a subject just to know about it, rather than to solve a problem—for example, understanding the doctrine of the last times, questioning the phenomenon of photosynthesis or the nature of the cosmos. Pursuing an opinion in order to determine its features, advantages or disadvantages. Continuous learning. This is usually an academic talent closely tied to scholarship. It closely resembles the quest-to-know discussed in Proverbs.

No   Yes

51. *Appraising and Estimating?*
1 2 3 4 5

Assessing the monetary value of, for example, a house, car, antique, collectable, business opportunity, financial investment and the like. Bargain hunting. People with this talent are often able to project future outcomes and financial return, so they serve well as investment buyers or financial and business consultants. Ministry organizations need this talent in order to make good purchasing and property and equipment decisions.

52. *Synthesizing?*
1 2 3 4 5

Putting together different or seemingly unrelated parts in order to make a whole, as in a project, report or book. Selecting ideas, concepts or objects in order to fit them together in a useful way. Being eclectic.

Making Decisions

The ability to act instinctively with limited information by being decisive or by taking risks, especially in an emergency situation. You may have one, two or none of these talents as strengths.

53. *Quick Reflex?*
1 2 3 4 5

Quickly and skillfully responding to emergency or accident situations, such as a child choking, auto accident, kitchen fire, person drowning with little pre-thought. Also quick reflexes and decision making during sporting events, military or police action or live broadcasts.

54. *Taking Risks?*
1 2 3 4 5

Willingness to make decisions risking your time, resources or finances when there is a significant chance of failure—often in business ventures, investing or trying something new.

Review your highest numerical scores above and select your three to five strongest talents. If this is a difficult selection for you, you have the option to complete the more in-depth IDAK online Natural Talent assessment at *IDAKgroup.com/tdg*.

1. _____

2. _____

3. _____

4. _____

5. _____

You have just completed the third and final talent assessment exercise. You will use these findings in the next chapter (Chapter 6), in Exercise Eight.

In Chapter 6 you'll begin to consolidate what you've discovered in your self-exploration and allow it to direct you toward your ideal task.

Chapter 6
Zeroing in on Your Task

Mike, now in his late thirties, was employed for ten years as a middle manager for a company that designed, manufactured and installed rain water processing units for commercial buildings, parking lots and road projects. His company was bought out, and the new corporate owner's priority of profit over customer service didn't allow Mike to ensure that the water processing units were installed correctly. His schedule became a continual source of frustration—too much work and too little time. Eventually, Mike left the company.

Close to a year went by, and Mike was unable to satisfy his personal passion in other lines of work. So he became my (John's) client. He wanted to follow his calling and at the same time receive compensation comparable to that of his former position. His self-evaluation exercises turned up a personal passion and natural talents compatible with several career options. One possible match Mike considered was working with international disaster relief organizations. He faithfully pursued his research into this type of organization and visited one that was based near his city. Much to his surprise, he discovered a special kinship there—these were his type of people.

He met with senior department heads, and one director commented on the availability of a mid-management position coming open because its current occupant was being promoted. The position involved overseeing mobile dental clinics in his city and surrounding rural areas. Would Mike be interested in looking at that opportunity? Mike had never done anything like this before, yet after we evaluated the job description, he and I came to a clear consensus that the organization fit his passion and the job duties fit his natural talents. He learned that he was up against other applicants who had experience in the job duties, but God's favor was upon him and he was selected above the others.

This was a dream come true for Mike—an opportunity to serve in ministry while also performing a job that fit his talent strengths, a job at which he could thrive. Would he ever have thought to pursue this dream position if he hadn't stopped to evaluate his personal passion and his natural talents? Probably not. Discovery of his passion and gifting paved his path, the way you are now paving your path toward your best team and task.

Job Matches, Good and Bad

You recall that in Chapter 2 you used your personal passion as a "filter" to begin selecting like-minded organizations. Similarly, in this chapter you will consolidate your God-given talent strengths (from Chapters 3, 4 and 5) into one *Summary Task Definition*, which you will use to filter and find your optimum job duties. In other words, you will match your talents to the tasks that maximize your strengths, bringing you greatest fulfillment and making greatest eternal impact for God's kingdom.

Match your talents to the tasks that maximize your strenghts.

Now, maybe you've already been capitalizing on your strengths in your career. If so, you've been enjoying yourself for a long time. Sometimes you've even marveled that you get paid to do your job. For those whose present work fits their strengths, it's likely that the tasks involved in your future ministry job will be similar to the tasks you've already been doing.

But what if you've been struggling, trying to thrive in a job for which you aren't well matched? Don't assume that just because you've been doing a task for the last twenty years, it's what you should also do in the future. If you've been living for years with tension and stress, why would you perpetuate more of the same?

Following is a list of telltale signs of a bad fit. We all exhibit some of these symptoms from time to time. But when a cluster of them forms a significant, ongoing pattern, it indicates that you probably haven't been doing tasks that make the most of your talent strengths.

Someone whose job predominantly involves tasks for which they are poorly matched is likely to be...
- Consistently tired—perhaps to the point of burnout.
- Frustrated by lack of achievement.
- Discouraged because they have tried so hard and have little to show for it.
- Lacking in job satisfaction, even when performing well.
- Prone to unprecedented mistakes.
- Working harder, not smarter; getting less done in more time.
- Avoiding work relationships that go beneath the surface.
- Obsessed with impressing others rather than enjoying a job well done.
- Lacking the support and approval of coworkers and even spouse.

These symptoms draw their life-draining power from three root trouble sources. The first is a *distorted self-concept.* An inaccurate or inadequate self-concept—especially when it involves a misperception of our natural talents—can cause us to set unrealistic ambitions for ourselves. Then, when we unsuccessfully pursue unrealistic goals, we may end up further distorting our self-concept. So this particular trouble source crops up both at the root and in the fruit of unrealistic ambition.

The second and third trouble sources—*the excessive energy required to keep up with others* and *fear of failure*—feed on each other. The more energy we have to put into a task that doesn't come naturally to us, the more we fear failing at it; the more we fear failure, the harder we work to stave it off. Ducks do not work hard at swimming, but an eagle trying to swim works very hard indeed, because it is badly matched to that task. When we're operating at a frenetic energy level just to stay afloat, we need to ask ourselves if we've made a bad match between our ambitions and our talents in our present career.

Attempting to transition into a new ministry role that uses the same poorly matched job skills makes just as little sense. Yet too many ministry organizations are quick to recruit one's past occupational experience without considering whether the related skills match one's God-given talents. Too often we have heard, "Oh, you are a teacher; we really need one of those," with no consideration as to whether or not the person was ever genuinely gifted to teach. Such a man or woman may have spent fifteen unhappy years teaching in public schools, struggling to succeed without the natural talent for classroom instruction. Then he or she transitions into a new teaching role in ministry. Guess what will probably happen? Whereas a naturally gifted teacher would intuitively adapt his or her past experience to the unique present job task, the teacher who is *not* naturally gifted will founder in the new situation, unable to draw upon any hard-won past experience. Teaching is simply not in their blood.

Evaluate Your Stress Level: The Sixty-Forty Principle

So...when you engage in a job that makes good use of your natural talents, your work becomes stress-free, right? Well, not exactly.

First, understand that not all stress is bad. In recent decades, innovative thinkers have distinguished between what they've termed *eustress* (good stress) and *distress* (bad stress). You can recognize healthy stress growing in you when you encounter a reasonable degree of competitiveness, an occasional failure (or the prospect of possible failure), or that periodic dose of adrenaline when you're up against a deadline.

You can find a job that minimizes your stress to a healthy level.

And second, every job requires that we perform some tasks that aren't matched to our strengths. Even when you've found a job that makes good use of your natural talents, you should expect some times of frustration and some stressful activities. Such difficulties are a normal and inevitable part of life. You can't eliminate all the stresses from any job. But you can find a job that minimizes your stress to a healthy level, a job in which your primary activities are enjoyable and fulfilling.

As a way to evaluate your present and future ministry job fit, we suggest the sixty-forty rule: *In the performance of your job duties, to thrive you must spend at least 60 percent of your time using your talent strengths, and no more than 40 percent of your time in areas of non-strength.* We are able to put up with the mundane tasks if most of our work is energizing. We are strengthened by operating in our strengths, depleted by operating in areas for which we are not wired.

Your personal collection of non-strengths do not excuse you from inadequate performance in activities that don't come naturally to you. Life teaches that lesson. We're not all gifted to be supervisors, and yet most of us have children who need our supervision. Similarly, musicians sometimes need to order their space, accountants sometimes need to show compassion, and CEOs sometimes need to take out the garbage.

The Servant Quotient

The bottom line: No matter what our gifting, God calls all of us to come to our ministry roles with the same attitude—the attitude of Christ, "who...made Himself of no reputation, taking the form of a bondservant, and...humbled Himself and became obedient to the point of death" (Philippians 2:6-8).

Often in my role as founder and workshop leader with Finishers Project, I (Nelson) am asked what it takes to have a successful ministry experience. My reply is: "Be willing to come to serve. Be willing to take the last seat at the table. Even though your experience and talent might enable you to run circles around everyone else, choose the humble position, and wait to see whether others will invite you up to some position of prominence and more responsibility."

Be willing to take the last seat at the table.

Invariably people respond, "Thank you for telling me that."

Don't come into a ministry saying, "No, no, no, you're doing it all wrong." Come with a servant leader mindset. Get ready to wash some feet .

David was a leader in a large New England church and a talented oral surgeon. He gave up his practice to serve in a Latin American country. Although David and is wife were used to living large, they were determined to have a successful ministry career, starting out at the bottom of the ladder in their field assignment.

These principles are at the foundation of your future success.

They took a huge voluntary step down in status to serve in their new place. But they accepted their circumstances with a smile and hearts of servants.

He could have strolled into the field assignment, saying, "Hey, the talent has arrived. We need to make some changes around here." But instead he cheerfully submitted to performing his given task, fitting in with the organization's existing ways of doing things.

Someone who knew his reputation came to him and asked, "Why are you behaving like a new intern here? Shouldn't you be in charge?"

"I'm just contributing where I'm asked to serve," he replied.

That was how David started in his ministry job. And the Lord honored him. David and his wife ended up becoming field leaders, making a tremendous impact for good. He later started a very creative ministry, MedSend, raising money to pay down the debts of recent medical school graduates while they serve their first few professional years in needy parts of the world. Not only does David's ministry address the physical needs of thousands around the world, but all of these new doctors enjoy a life-shaping experience overseas before they become tied down with a family and a practice.

No Lone Rangers

You may think we've strayed from our purpose in this chapter, talking about servanthood and job stress. But these principles are part of the mindset you need as you select your ideal task and your ideal team. They're at the foundation of your future success—the attitudinal ground on which you will walk.

In a similar vein, before we move on, we want to address two more foundational issues that relate to your selection of your team. First, among the handful of nonnegotiable convictions we hold, both of us believe firmly in the centrality of the local church in any ministry effort. The local church is where we are honed, polished, developed and matured. It's where many of our most important relationships are established and where we find the ongoing support, equipping and accountability necessary for ministry success. If you want to maximize your potential in service, you must be actively and intimately involved in a local church. And in many cases, your ministry should function as an extension of your church relationships with fellow members and even pastoral leaders. Your church is your home team that provides the critical support and accountability for what you are doing—assuming, of course, they are in active agreement with Christ's Great Commission. (If they're not, go find a home church that is.)

And second, we've found that your ministry success is most assured when you serve as part of an established organization, rather than launching out on your own. In the past, the world needed individuals and small groups to pioneer new ministries, both locally and globally. But today ministry organizations exist in an astounding number of specialized niches in most parts of the world. Today we find that the need for individual bootstraps efforts is rare. Even if your passion and gifting are leading you to do something cutting-edge new, we advise you to first learn the ropes with an experienced existing organization. Then, if it makes sense, branch out on your own. However, you will usually best steward your time and resources when you help advance the existing efforts of organizations that are already involved in your areas of interest.

Exercise Eight
Defining Your Ideal Task

It's time to pull together all of the exercises you have completed in chapters 3–5 and consolidate them into one *Summary Task Definition*. Then, in the next exercise, you'll use this definition as a filter to identify types of job positions that fit you best.

1. Review the *Communicational* talent or talents you identified at the end of Exercise Five in Chapter 3 and complete this sentence:

    I believe God has gifted me to communicate (in all situations, but especially in communicating His love) using the following Communicational talent strength or strengths...

    a. _____

    b. _____

    c. _____

2. Review the *Relational* talent that you identified at the end of Exercise Six in Chapter 4 and complete this sentence:

    I believe God has gifted me with the ability to relate to others best as a...

    _____

3. Review the *Functional* talents you identified at the end of Exercise Seven in Chapter 5 and complete this sentence:

    I believe God has gifted me with the following functional talents, any of which could be the core of my future ministry job duty. I can best serve others by...

    a. _____

    b. _____

c. _____

d. _____

e. _____

4. Bring together your talent strengths from 1–3 above to complete the following *Summary Task Definition.* You may wish to use your own words, rather than our names for your talents.

Your Summary Task Definition

My ideal ministry task involves **communicating** *by or through*

[Communicational talent(s)]_____

_____

in a [Relational talent] _____ **relational environment,**

doing [Functional talents]_____

_____

_____

Important: You've identified at least five and as many as nine total talent strengths that you possess. As we move ahead, please understand that any one job will make use of a maximum of four of your identified talents. In other words, there's no job that will make use of all of your identified talent strengths. So, for example, you might find a job that draws upon two of your *Communicational* talents, your one *Relational* talent and one of your *Functional* talents. Or the core of your future job might make use of one *Communicational,* one *Relational* and two *Functional* talents. This understanding will help you make realistic selections in Exercise Nine.

Exercise Nine
Your Optimum Ministry Job Duties

In this exercise you're going to perform a three-stage screening of the job duties in the following list, using your identified talent strengths as your "filters."

1. First, review your *Communicational* talent strength (or strengths) listed above. In the list of job duties below, write the letter *C* in the space beside any job duties that may use one or two of your *Communicational* talents. You should end up marking many of the items with *C*.

2. Next, go through the list again, this time writing the letter *R* in the space beside the job duties that affirm and employ your *Relational* talent. Do you perform best when you encounter many new faces every day? Or when you work with one or two individuals for a long time? Or with a medium-sized group of familiar friends? Try to picture how many new people would be in your immediate work environment for each job, and then determine whether this is a match for your *Relational* talent.

3. Finally, review your *Functional* talents above and use these for your third step of screening. Write the letter *F* beside job duties that best use any one or two of your *Functional* talents.

_____ Accounting, financial, bookkeeping duties
_____ Advertising, marketing duties
_____ Advocacy, lobbying duties
_____ Agricultural labor duties
_____ Animal care, training duties
_____ Appraising, estimating duties
_____ Broadcasting duties
_____ Childcare duties
_____ Church planting duties
_____ Cooking, meal preparation duties
_____ Computer systems duties
_____ Construction duties
_____ Consulting duties
_____ Counseling, mental health duties
_____ Custodial, cleaning duties
_____ Designing duties
_____ Disaster aid duties
_____ Discipling duties
_____ Education administration duties
_____ Elder or disabled care duties
_____ Employee or member care duties
_____ Engineering duties
_____ Entrepreneur duties

_____ Equipment operational duties

_____ Evangelizing duties

_____ Event or meeting scheduling duties

_____ Factory, assembly line duties

_____ Food or supply distribution duties

_____ Fundraising duties

_____ General labor duties

_____ Graphic arts duties

_____ Guarding, protecting duties

_____ Health care assistant duties

_____ Health care professional duties

_____ Hospitality, restaurant service duties

_____ Inspection, investigation duties

_____ Legal, legal assistance duties

_____ Management, executive duties

_____ Mechanical and technical operational duties

_____ Mediating, conflict resolution duties

_____ Mentoring duties

_____ Performing arts (music, drama, dance) duties

_____ Office administration duties

_____ Pastoring duties

_____ Preaching, speaking duties

_____ Public relations duties

_____ Quality control duties

_____ Reception, secretarial duties

_____ Recruitment duties

_____ Records management duties

_____ Rescuing duties

_____ Research and development duties

_____ Research (information) duties

_____ Repair, installation (electronics, appliance) duties

_____ Repair, installation (machinery, vehicle) duties

_____ Retail or grocery store duties

_____ Sales duties

_____ Salvaging, recycling duties

_____ Social service duties

_____ Sports, recreation duties

_____ Storage, warehousing duties

_____ Teaching (classroom) duties

_____ Therapy (physical, occupational, speech) duties

_____ Training, instructing duties

_____ Transportation (land, water, air) duties

_____ Translating duties

_____ Tutoring (academic) duties

_____ Tutoring life skills duties

_____ Typing, transcription duties

_____ Veterinary medicine duties

_____ Visual arts (painting, drawing, sculpture, video) duties

_____ Writing, editing duties

_____ Other (specify:) _____

_____duties

_____ Other (specify:) _____

_____duties

4. Once you've completed marking job duties with _C, R_ and _F,_ note especially the duties that you've labeled with all three letters. These are the job duties that are most likely to match your talent strengths. Select one or more list items that you've labeled with either two or three letters, and write these preferred job duties below.

_____ job duties

_____ job duties

_____ job duties

Now, you may thinking, *Hasn't some one figured out how to computerize this process?* Yes! As we've mentioned before, you're welcome to take advantage of the IDAK Career Match system, with over 90,000 career match combinations. You complete a paper-and-pencil self-assessment, and we process it and help you interpret and apply the results. You're welcome to inquire about and upgrade to the computer match at any time you wish.

*   *   *

Congratulations. You have finished using your talent strengths to narrow down your optimum job duties.

In Chapter 7 we'll help you further narrow your team selection, and we'll merge your optimum duties with a few well-matched ministry organization types, in preparation for you to find your best job working with your best team. You're now very close to discovering the specific niche God has set aside just for you.

Chapter 7
Zeroing in on Your Team

Pat grew up as a missionary kid in Papua New Guinea. When she moved with her parents to the United States, she entered college and studied finance and accounting. After graduation she landed a finance job.

After two years, Pat's entrepreneurial talent (*Initiating and Developing*, talent 24) and her *Solving Problems* talent (talent 46) began to feel neglected and raised their voices. So she made her first career transition, forming her own small business consulting firm. By instinct, she had moved into a situation where her job duties were now maximizing her natural talents.

After six years of successful consulting work, Pat still sensed that something was missing. This was her passion speaking up. She had grown up in a ministry environment and valued causes that would advance God's kingdom. But she had begun to feel that helping small businesses succeed was not directly contributing to her desire to serve God in ministry, especially when she was helping businesses whose product or service bore no relation to her personal passion. So Pat began to focus her consulting attention on helping ministry organizations become financially successful. Now she was performing job duties that were well matched to her gifting, and she was teaming up with organizations whose passion overlapped with hers.

Ultimately, a pregnancy resource ministry—which assists pregnant women through counseling and support to choose alternatives to abortion—recognized Pat's financial and problem solving intuition and offered her a full-time job. Pat accepted. She also volunteered her time with a downtown street mission that focused on recovery for victims of alcohol and drug abuse.

Over a period of two years, Pat's succeeded at cleaning up the financial issues of her pregnancy resource ministry. Now she found herself performing the more mundane duties of maintaining the organization's finances, rather than breaking new ground and solving problems. She began looking for new challenges. This is when she came to IDAK and I (John) helped her through testing and counseling. Pat discovered that her volunteer work—assisting men and women recover from drug and alcohol addiction—truly fit her lifelong passion, and that her talents could be utilized in designing rehabilitation curriculum. After much prayer and conversation with the president of the recovery ministry where she volunteered her time, she negotiated a full-time position as director of education. She also continued in a volunteer consulting role with the pregnancy resource ministry, which amply satisfied the ongoing need there and allowed her to continue investing in a ministry that had captured part of her heart.

Pat's volunteer work fit her lifelong passion.

Pat had come full circle in her ministry search. She ended up choosing two ministry organizations that fit her passion, filling a primary job position that fit her talents.

Nearing the Goal

In this chapter you will come within a step or two of similarly completing your journey. Exercise Ten will help you match the ministry organization of your passion with the job duties which represent your strengths. Once you have pulled these two important parts of your future ministry together, in the next chapter you will learn how to confidently call or visit a ministry organization to validate your search.

And yes, if Exercise Ten is overwhelming or frustrating to you, for a list of organizations in the US that fit your strengths, you can go directly to ***ministrywebdirectory.com*** and complete the search for a ministry organization and receive a Primary Search Report. This is an exercise that serves the same purpose but leaves the processing work to the online computer.

Exercise Ten
Matching a Team to Your Task

Way back in Chapter 2, you worked through two exercises to discern your personal passion, and then you used your passion to begin narrowing possible categories of organizations that might share your passion. Now, in this exercise you will continue that narrowing process, using your personal passion to further narrow the types of organizations that are likely to share your passion.

Take a few minutes to review your responses in Exercises One and Two (in Chapter 2), to remind yourself what you learned about your personal passion. Keep this snapshot of your passion in mind as you continue.

The lists below are expanded from the lists in Exercise Three (end of Chapter 2). (The list items in Exercise Three are the same as the bold category headings in the lists below.) Review the lists below, marking each department or organization type that appeals to your personal passion—in other words, individuals within this ministry are likely to share your passion and partner with you in addressing it. You might give special attention to the categories you selected in Exercise Three, but scan over all other categories for individual items that appeal to you.

Church Departments & Church Programs

Select one, two or three departments or programs that appeal to you—that match well with your passion. If you do not find anything that fits your passion, consider possibly starting a ministry in your church with another person.

SUPPORT SERVICES
CHURCH DEPARTMENTS
- ❑ Food closet
- ❑ Graphic design
- ❑ Information technology
- ❑ Marketing, promotion
- ❑ Bulletin, newsletter, magazine

- ❑ Office administration
- ❑ Purchasing
- ❑ Storage, warehouse
- ❑ Transportation
- ❑ Ushering, greeting
- ❑ Parking
- ❑ Website
- ❑ Research

COUNSELING, CAREGIVING
CHURCH DEPARTMENTS
- ❑ Caregiving
- ❑ Counseling
- ❑ Crisis intervention
- ❑ Elderly caregiving
- ❑ Homeless shelter
- ❑ Meals, home repair
- ❑ Peer counseling

- ❏ Pregnancy counseling
- ❏ Recovery support groups
- ❏ Visitation

EVANGELISM, OUTREACH
CHURCH DEPARTMENTS
- ❏ Campus outreach
- ❏ City government outreach
- ❏ Community development
- ❏ Ethnic, multicultural
- ❏ Evangelism
- ❏ Inner city outreach
- ❏ International students
- ❏ Military
- ❏ Global missions
- ❏ Prison
- ❏ Short-term mission teams

LEADERSHIP, MANAGEMENT
CHURCH DEPARTMENTS
- ❏ Capital campaign management
- ❏ Church planting
- ❏ Deacon board
- ❏ Elder board
- ❏ Finance, tax
- ❏ Lay leadership management
- ❏ Leadership training
- ❏ Legal counsel
- ❏ Ministry partnerships
- ❏ Human resources

- ❏ Internal administration
- ❏ Mobilization, assimilation
- ❏ New vision committee
- ❏ Prayer team

MUSIC, ART, DRAMA
CHURCH DEPARTMENTS
- ❏ Artistic expression
- ❏ Choir
- ❏ Contemporary worship team
- ❏ Drama group
- ❏ Media production
- ❏ Music group
- ❏ Music, worship team
- ❏ Orchestra, band
- ❏ Radio broadcast
- ❏ Piano, keyboard

OPERATIONS, FACILITIES
CHURCH DEPARTMENTS
- ❏ Audiovisual equipment
- ❏ Buildings & grounds
- ❏ Hospitality, coffee service
- ❏ Décor, interior design
- ❏ Flower arranging
- ❏ Food service
- ❏ Sanctuary lighting

RECREATION, EVENTS
CHURCH DEPARTMENTS
- ❏ Auctions
- ❏ Camp

- ❏ Campouts
- ❏ Children's events
- ❏ Potlucks
- ❏ Sports tournaments
- ❏ Event administration
- ❏ Event planning
- ❏ Retreats

TEACHING, DISCIPLING
CHURCH DEPARTMENTS
- ❏ Adult ministry
- ❏ Advocacy committee
- ❏ Bookstore
- ❏ Children's ministry
- ❏ Church seminary
- ❏ College ministry
- ❏ Disabled, handicapped ministry
- ❏ Discipleship
- ❏ Financial stewardship
- ❏ Home study groups
- ❏ Infants
- ❏ Library
- ❏ Marriage, family
- ❏ Men's ministry
- ❏ New member orientation
- ❏ Preschool, daycare
- ❏ Public policy awareness
- ❏ Single's ministry
- ❏ Special needs
- ❏ Summer children's programs
- ❏ Women's ministry
- ❏ Youth ministry

Local and Global Ministry Organizations with Classification Numbers

Select at least three, but no more than five ministry organization categories. The classification numbers will help in Exercise Eleven, when you go to the web to search for names of ministry organizations.

Advertising, Arts & Cultural Organizations
❏ Advertising, publicity organizations (7310)
❏ Advertising organizations (7311)
❏ Graphic design, graphic arts organizations (7312)

Advocacy, Human Rights, Political Organizations
❏ Advocacy, reform, justice, political change organizations (7313)
❏ Church-sponsored advocacy, political awareness (8442)
❏ Environmental concerns organizations (8556)

Agriculture & Livestock Support Organizations
❏ Agriculture support, crop farm service organizations (1010)
❏ Farming consulting organizations (1011)
❏ Tree, fruit, nut farming organizations (1012)
❏ Grain, vegetable farming organizations (1013)
❏ Seed, fertilizer supply organizations (1014)
❏ Forest, nursery stock farming organizations (1015)
❏ Farming equipment, tools, supply organizations (1016)
❏ Tree harvesting, trimming organizations (1017)
❏ Sawmill organizations (1020)
❏ Livestock, fish, poultry farming organizations (1030)
❏ Livestock consulting organizations (1031)
❏ Livestock farming, ranching organizations (1032)
❏ Horse farming, ranching organizations (1033)
❏ Poultry, egg farming organizations (1034)
❏ Dairy farming organizations (1035)
❏ Animal feed supply organizations (1036)
❏ Animal, boarding, grooming organizations (1037)
❏ Veterinary services organizations (1050)
❏ Veterinary clinics, hospitals (1051)
❏ Veterinary medicine, supply organizations (1052)

Children Services & Outreach Organizations
❏ Child care, day schools (8215)
❏ Social service organizations (8320)
❏ Adoption service organizations (8321)
❏ Orphanages (8322)
❏ Foster care organizations (8325)
❏ Child protection, rescue service organizations (8348)
❏ Child evangelism, outreach organizations (8381)
❏ Church-sponsored outreach to homeless, street youth (8419)
❏ Church-sponsored shelters for women, children (8429)
❏ Church-sponsored day school, day care centers (8433)

Church, Church Consulting, Support Organizations

❏ Church, building construction organizations (1510)
❏ Church, architectural design organizations (1511)
❏ Church construction organizations (1512)
❏ Churches, denominations (8400)
❏ Denominations (8401)
❏ Churches, metro or urban (8402)
❏ Churches, rural (8403)
❏ Churches, inner city (8404)
❏ Churches, suburban (8405)
❏ Church planting organizations (8406)
❏ Church growth, consulting organizations (8407)
❏ Church-sponsored outreach to Inner City (8411)
❏ Church-sponsored outreach to ethnic, minority groups (8412)
❏ Church-sponsored outreach to men (8413)
❏ Church-sponsored outreach to women (8414)
❏ Church-sponsored outreach to college students (8415)
❏ Church-sponsored outreach to disabled, handicapped (8416)
❏ Church-sponsored outreach to seniors (8417)
❏ Church-sponsored outreach to jail, prison inmates (8418)
❏ Church-sponsored outreach to homeless, street youth (8419)
❏ Church-sponsored church planting programs (8421)
❏ Church-sponsored outreach to schools (8422)
❏ Church-sponsored community service outreach (8423)
❏ Church-sponsored public works programs (8424)
❏ Church-sponsored medical, dental service programs (8425)
❏ Church-sponsored community transportation programs (8426)
❏ Church-sponsored clothing, food distribution programs (8427)
❏ Church-sponsored refugee, immigrant programs (8428)
❏ Church-sponsored shelters for women, children (8429)
❏ Church-sponsored counseling offices (8431)
❏ Church-sponsored K-12 schools (8432)
❏ Church-sponsored day school, day care centers (8433)
❏ Church-sponsored colleges, seminaries (8434)
❏ Church-sponsored outreach to marketplace (8435)
❏ Church-sponsored crisis intervention programs (8436)
❏ Church-sponsored global church planting (8437)
❏ Church-sponsored arts, drama, music performances (8438)
❏ Church-sponsored prayer outreach (8439)
❏ Church-sponsored publications (8441)
❏ Church-sponsored advocacy, political awareness (8442)
❏ Church-sponsored employment, career assistance (8443)
❏ Church-sponsored community evangelism programs (8444)
❏ Church-sponsored family, marriage programs (8445)
❏ Church-sponsored temporary, low-cost housing (8446)
❏ Church-sponsored broadcast programs (8447)
❏ Church-sponsored senior housing (8448)

❏ Church-sponsored outreach to college athletes (8449)

Community Development, Construction & Maintenance
❏ Building, plant construction organizations (1513)
❏ Residential construction organizations (1514)
❏ Large building construction organizations (1515)
❏ Emergency shelter construction, assembly organizations (1516)
❏ Construction, subcontracting organizations (1700)
❏ Highway, road construction organizations (1701)
❏ Bridge, tunnel construction organizations (1702)
❏ Water, sewer, pipeline construction organizations (1703)
❏ Power line, gas, cable, construction organizations (1704)
❏ Waste water, treatment plant construction organizations (1705)
❏ Oil pipeline, refinery construction organizations (1706)
❏ Dam construction, flood control construction organizations (1707)
❏ Marine, harbor construction organizations (1708)
❏ Power plant construction organizations (1709)
❏ Railway construction organizations (1711)
❏ Air terminal construction organizations (1712)
❏ Recycle plant construction organizations (1713)
❏ Subcontracting construction organizations (1770)
❏ Plumbing, heating, AC construction organizations (1771)
❏ Painting contractor organizations (1772)

❏ Electrical contractor organizations (1773)
❏ Masonry, insulation, dry wall, plaster organizations (1774)
❏ Carpentry, flooring contracting organizations (1775)
❏ Roofing, siding, sheet metal contracting organizations (1776)
❏ Concrete contracting organizations (1777)
❏ Structural steel erection organizations (1778)
❏ Well drilling, excavation, demolition service organizations (1780)
❏ Excavation organizations (1781)
❏ Demolition, minefield removal organizations (1782)
❏ Church-sponsored public works programs (8424)
❏ Environmental concerns organizations (8556)

Computer & Related Technology Service Organizations
❏ Internet Service Provider organizations (4820)
❏ Computer, data processing services organizations (7370)

Consulting & Legal Services Organizations
❏ Legal services organizations (8111)
❏ Management, personnel consulting service organizations (8553)
❏ Leadership, training services organizations (8554)
❏ Environmental concerns organizations (8556)

Counseling, Residential Recovery Organizations
❏ Mental health care residential establishments (8071)
❏ Hospice care organizations (8327)

- ❏ Counseling services organizations (8330)
- ❏ Drug, alcohol treatment services organizations (8331)
- ❏ Learning disabilities assessment organizations (8332)
- ❏ Marriage, family counseling service organizations (8333)
- ❏ Financial debt counseling organizations (8334)
- ❏ Addiction counseling, recovery organizations (8335)
- ❏ Residency recovery counseling organizations (8336)
- ❏ Career, vocational counseling organizations (8337)
- ❏ Life coaching, business coaching service organizations (8338)
- ❏ Crisis intervention (recovery) organizations (8340)
- ❏ Juvenile correction services establishments (8342)
- ❏ Homosexual, lesbian outreach organizations (8345)
- ❏ Reconciliation (including racial) organizations (8346)
- ❏ Church-sponsored counseling offices (8431)
- ❏ Military chaplaincies (armed forces) (8555)

Crisis Intervention & Disaster Relief Organizations

- ❏ Chaplaincy service organizations (nonmilitary) (8324)
- ❏ Drug, alcohol treatment services organizations (8331)
- ❏ Addiction counseling, recovery organizations (8335)
- ❏ Crisis intervention (recovery) organizations (8340)
- ❏ Inner city, rescue organizations & establishments (8341)
- ❏ Juvenile correction services establishments (8342)

- ❏ Women's intervention, pregnancy counseling establishments (8343)
- ❏ Prison, correctional rehab service establishments (8344)
- ❏ Homosexual, lesbian outreach organizations (8345)
- ❏ Prisoner, ex-offender outreach organizations (8347)
- ❏ Child protection, rescue services organizations (8348)
- ❏ Disaster, relief organizations (8350)
- ❏ Church-sponsored outreach to homeless, street youth (8419)
- ❏ Church-sponsored crisis intervention programs (8436)

Disabled Services & Outreach Organizations

- ❏ Disabled, handicapped residential care establishments (8063)
- ❏ Disabled, handicapped evangelism or outreach (8392)
- ❏ Church-sponsored outreach to disabled, handicapped (8416)

Discipleship & Prayer Organizations

- ❏ Prayer outreach organizations (8386)
- ❏ Discipleship, small group ministry organizations (8395)
- ❏ Church-sponsored prayer outreach (8439)

Distribution Service Organizations

- ❏ Distribution service organizations (5000)
- ❏ Auto, vehicle, equipment parts distribution organizations (5010)
- ❏ Lumber, building materials distribution organizations (5030)
- ❏ Computer, office equipment, supplies distribution organizations (5040)
- ❏ Medical, dental, hospital supplies distribution organizations (5050)

❏ Misc. Equipment, supplies distribution organizations (5060)
❏ Music, video media distribution organizations (5090)
❏ Medical drug, soaps, toiletries distribution organizations (5120)
❏ Clothing, used clothing distribution organizations (5130)
❏ Import, export native handcraft distribution organizations (5131)
❏ Food, beverage distribution organizations (5140)
❏ Book, printed material distribution organizations (5191)
❏ Survival kits & materials distribution organizations (5199)
❏ Printed music distribution organizations (7391)
❏ Church-sponsored clothing, food distribution programs (8427)

Education & Literacy Organizations
❏ Schools, elementary, secondary (8211)
❏ Schools, physically handicapped, elementary, secondary (8212)
❏ Home school support organizations (8213)
❏ Child care, day schools (8215)
❏ Sunday school associations (8216)
❏ Day school, Sunday school associations (8217)
❏ Colleges, seminaries (8220)
❏ Colleges, universities, not Christian (8222)
❏ Colleges, Christian (8223)
❏ Colleges, Bible (8224)
❏ Online colleges, correspondence colleges (8225)
❏ Seminaries, graduate schools (8226)
❏ Flight training schools (8227)
❏ Library & information service organizations (8231)

❏ English as second language organizations (8232)
❏ Literacy, special ed organizations (8233)
❏ Mentoring (educational) organizations (8234)
❏ Church-sponsored outreach to schools (8422)
❏ Church-sponsored K-12 schools (8432)
❏ Church-sponsored day school, day care centers (8433)
❏ Church-sponsored colleges, seminaries (8434)
❏ Leadership, training service organizations (8554)

Employment Mobilization, Referral Organizations
❏ Personnel, referral, placement, mobilization organizations (7360)
❏ Career, vocational counseling organizations (8337)
❏ Church-sponsored employment, career assistance (8443)

Evangelism Organizations
❏ Marketplace outreach organizations (8360)
❏ Men's outreach or seminar organizations (8361)
❏ Women's outreach or seminar organizations (8362)
❏ Child, youth, campus evangelism or outreach organizations (8380)
❏ Child evangelism or outreach organizations (8381)
❏ Youth evangelism or outreach organizations (8382)
❏ Campus evangelism or outreach organizations (8383)
❏ International student outreach organizations (8384)
❏ Athletes, sports outreach organizations (8385)

❏ Evangelism, outreach organizations (8390)

❏ Family evangelism or outreach organizations (8391)

❏ Disabled, handicapped evangelism or outreach (8392)

❏ Military evangelism or outreach organizations (8393)

❏ Evangelistic crusade organizations (8394)

❏ Church-sponsored outreach to college students (8415)

❏ Church-sponsored community evangelism programs (8444)

Family & Marriage Concerns Organizations

❏ Social service organizations (8320)

❏ Marriage, family counseling service organizations (8333)

❏ Financial debt counseling organizations (8334)

❏ Family evangelism or outreach organizations (8391)

❏ Church-sponsored family, marriage programs (8445)

Financial Aid & Business Development Organizations

❏ Business start-up loan, economic aid organizations (6153)

❏ Fundraising service organizations (6281)

❏ Financial planning, stewardship, development organizations (6282)

❏ Financial consulting service organizations (6283)

❏ Insurance (ministry based) organizations (6310)

❏ Life insurance (ministry service) organizations (6311)

❏ Retirement, pension fund organizations (6371)

❏ Equipment leasing, rental organizations (7350)

Foundations, Trusts & Membership Organizations

❏ Religious trusts, foundations (6732)

❏ Membership organizations (8370)

❏ Ministry membership organizations (8371)

❏ Theological societies, membership associations (8372)

❏ Global ministry membership organizations (8373)

❏ Professional membership organizations (8374)

❏ Educational membership organizations (8375)

❏ Educational support membership, consulting organizations (8376)

❏ Church membership associations (8377)

Hospitality & Boarding Service Organizations

❏ Lodging establishments (7010)

❏ Hotels, motels, guest house establishments (7011)

❏ Conference centers, resorts, retreats (7012)

❏ Hospitality, dormitory, boarding establishments (7013)

❏ Church-sponsored senior housing (8448)

Immigrant & Refugee Service Organizations

❏ Temporary, low cost housing organizations (7016)

❏ Public health education centers, service organizations (8013)

❏ English as second language organizations (8232)

❏ Literacy, special ed organizations (8233)

❏ Disaster, relief organizations (8350)

❏ International student outreach organizations (8384)

❏ Church-sponsored refugee, immigrant programs (8428)

Jail & Prison Outreach Organizations

❏ Juvenile correction services establishments (8342)

❏ Prison, correctional rehab services establishments (8344)

❏ Prisoner, ex-offender outreach organizations (8347)

❏ Church-sponsored outreach to jail, prison inmates (8418)

❏ Marketplace Outreach Organizations

❏ Business start-up loan, economic aid organizations (6153)

❏ Chaplaincy service organizations (nonmilitary) (8324)

❏ Life coaching, business coaching service organizations (8338)

❏ Marketplace outreach organizations (8360)

❏ Business women & men outreach organizations (8363)

❏ Discipleship, small group ministry organizations (8395)

❏ Church-sponsored outreach to marketplace (8435)

❏ Management, personnel consulting service organizations (8553)

❏ Leadership, training services organizations (8554)

Mechanical & Technical Repair Organizations

❏ Auto, mechanical repair services organizations (7511)

❏ Electrical repair services organizations (7515)

Media, Broadcasting & Publicity Organizations

❏ Broadcasting communication organizations (4810)

❏ Radio broadcasting stations (4811)

❏ TV broadcasting stations (4812)

❏ TV cable service organizations (4813)

❏ Advertising organizations (7311)

❏ Public relations, event planning service organizations (7314)

❏ Motion picture, production organizations (7812)

❏ TV, video, film, DVD production organizations (7813)

❏ Music video production organizations (7814)

❏ Motion picture, video, DVD distribution organizations (7822)

❏ Drama, performing arts organizations (7922)

❏ Radio program production organizations (7924)

❏ Music performing organizations (7929)

❏ Church-sponsored broadcast programs (8447)

Medical, Dental & Health Service Organizations

❏ Medical, health, nutrition service organizations (8010)

❏ Medical clinics, treatment centers, service organizations (8011)

❏ Nutrition, education service organizations (8012)

❏ Public health education centers., service organizations (8013)

❏ Physical & other therapy clinics (8014)

❏ Prosthetics clinics, labs (8015)

❏ Dental services, clinics, mobile services (8020)

❏ Hospitals (8060)

❏ Ship hospitals (8062)

❏ Church-sponsored medical, dental service programs (8425)

Men's Concerns Organizations

❑ Men's outreach or seminar organizations (8361)
❑ Business women & men outreach organizations (8363)
❑ Church-sponsored outreach to men (8413)

Music & Drama Organizations

❑ Music publishing organizations (2703)
❑ Music, video media distribution organizations (5090)
❑ Music distribution organizations (7391)
❑ Music recording organizations (7392)
❑ Music video production organizations (7814)
❑ Motion picture, video, DVD distribution organizations (7822)
❑ Drama, performing arts organizations (7922)
❑ Music performing organizations (7929)
❑ Church-sponsored arts, drama, music performances (8438)

Publishing & Printing Organizations

❑ Publishing organizations (2700)
❑ Magazine & misc. publishing organizations (2701)
❑ Bible, book publishing organizations (2702)
❑ Music publishing organizations (2703)
❑ Printing, copying service organizations (2750)
❑ Church-sponsored publications (8441)

Recovery, Rehabilitation & Reconciliation Organizations

❑ Social service organizations (8320)
❑ Drug, alcohol treatment services organizations (8331)

❑ Women's intervention, pregnancy counseling establishments (8343)
❑ Homosexual, lesbian outreach organizations (8345)
❑ Reconciliation (including racial) organizations (8346)
❑ Prisoner, ex-offender outreach organizations (8347)
❑ Church-sponsored outreach to ethnic, minority groups (8412)

Research, Archaeological & Translation Organizations

❑ Translating, Bible translating service organizations (7380)
❑ Research, development organizations (8551)
❑ Archaeological, historical service organizations (8552)

Seniors & Retirement Organizations

❑ Retirement, nursing homes, eldercare organizations (8072)
❑ Senior outreach organizations (8323)
❑ Church-sponsored senior housing (8448)

Sports & Recreation Organizations

❑ Camps, sporting recreational establishments (7014)
❑ Campgrounds, RV parks (7015)
❑ Physical & other therapy clinics (8014)
❑ Athletes, sports outreach organizations (8385)
❑ Church-sponsored outreach to college athletes (8449)

Stores: Book, Thrift, Catalogue or Specialty

❑ Native handcraft specialty stores (5310)
❑ Clothing stores, thrifts (5600)
❑ Music & music equipment stores (5700)

❏ Coffee houses, cafés, restaurants (5800)
❏ Pharmacies, drug stores (5910)
❏ Used equipment stores (5932)
❏ Book stores, religious supply stores (5942)
❏ Catalogue, internet stores (5960)
❏ Purchasing service organizations (7397)

❏ Transportation related service organizations (4700)
❏ Travel agencies (4701)
❏ Short-term ministry, tour coordinating organizations (4702)
❏ Freight, cargo forwarding organizations (4731)
❏ Church-sponsored community transportation programs (8426)

Transportation Service Organizations
❏ Land passenger service transportation organizations (4100)
❏ Land freight transportation service organizations (4101)
❏ Water passenger transportation organizations (4400)
❏ Water freight transportation organizations (4401)
❏ Air passenger transportation organizations (4500)
❏ Air freight transportation organizations (4501)

Women's Concerns Organizations
❏ Hairdresser, salon establishments (7230)
❏ Women's intervention, pregnancy counseling establishments (8343)
❏ Women's outreach or seminar organizations (8362)
❏ Business women & men outreach organizations (8363)
❏ Church-sponsored outreach to women (8414)
❏ Church-sponsored shelters for women, children (8429)

1. **THE TEAM.** Review the items you marked from both the church and ministry organization lists. From both lists combined, select your top five, for now. (You can come back later and select more, if necessary.) List these and, where available, their classification (CONI) numbers in the first two columns of the table below. These should be the five types of church departments or organizations that most closely match your personal passion.

2. **THE TASK.** Now revisit the job duties you listed at the end of Exercise Nine (end of Chapter 6). Rewrite these job duties in the third column of the table below. You may find that you will repeat the same job duty for different ministry organizations.

THE TEAM *Preferred Church Departments, Local and Global Ministry Organizations*	CONI *number**	THE TASK *Your Optimum Job Duties (from Exercise Nine)*

*Use 8400 for churches, if not otherwise specified.

What you now have is the pairing together of your possible ministry organization types and your optimal job duties. You can use this to describe your future possible team-and-task combination. For example, "My ideal ministry job might be working with a social service organization (CONI 8320) performing consulting, discipling or teaching duties."

Will your optimal job duties be currently in demand in every organization on your list? Possibly not. But you now have the outlines of a comprehensive picture, and your ideal future niche most likely falls somewhere within its boundaries. Who knows? You might even persuade an organization that they need you to fill a position they never before knew they needed.

*   *   *

You're almost there! Next, in Chapter 8, you will begin researching specific organizations, making contact with them and validating what you've learned about your best-fit organizations and job titles.

Chapter 8
Watching the Miracle Happen

Now that you have selected several future ministry options in Exercise Ten (Chapter 7), what comes next may surprise you. Your next step is *not* to launch your search, trying to get a part-time or full-time position. First you're going to complete the final pre-search step, giving yourself and God a chance to validate or refine your selections of possible organizations and job duties. Then when you do actively begin pursuing your ministry niche, you'll do so with maximum confidence that your plans are well-matched to you.

Up to now, all of your evaluation has involved praying, reading and completing exercises that some might call paperwork. Your next step involves going out into the ministry headquarters or service locations, but not for the reasons you might think. Have you ever tried to select and buy a car after doing nothing but watch TV ads? Probably not. The advertisements might help you narrow your search, but at some point you go to the dealer, see the car "in person" and take it for a test drive. In fact, you probably test-drive several cars from multiple dealers before making your final choice. For similar reasons, your next step in following your calling is to take your new ministry selections—organization types and job duties—for a test drive to determine if you truly have a sense of bonding with the team and the task.

Yes, you're still exploring, but you're now exploring with a much clearer idea where to look and a much better chance of recognizing your perfect ministry role when you see it. You can confidently call or visit a ministry organization and spell out your heart's passion, your gifting and the specific task you seek to perform within that organization. This will streamline the search both for you and for the organization. For any recruitment manager or department director, your clear vision and your grounded self-assessment will be a breath of fresh air.

Courage is doing the right thing in spite of your fear.

So keep pressing to complete this final step. Keep listening to God and stay true to His leading. Which always means staying open to obedient risk. If you're feeling timid or nervous, that's normal. Courage isn't the absence of fear; it's doing the right thing in spite of your fear. Rely on God and He'll always enable you to do what's right. Actually, there is very little risk at this point. You are just test-driving the car; you've left your credit card and checkbook at home.

Following are a few basic thoughts about this test-drive phase. We'll guide you carefully through the details at the end of this chapter, in Exercise Eleven.

Discern by Direct Exposure

When Jesus evaluated and called His followers, He did it in person, looking the individual in the eye, conversing, sharing experiences over time. Your next step of following your calling must also involve personal, face-to-face exposure.

You need direct, hands-on exposure to at least one specific ministry organization for every organization type you selected at the end of Exercise Ten (Chapter 7). For example, if you selected "Disaster relief organizations (8350)," "Pregnancy counseling establishments (8343)" and "Adoption service organizations (8321)" as the types of ministries with whom you might serve, then this next step (Exercise Eleven) involves your contacting and visiting at least one of each ministry type. Your purpose in these visits is to validate or refine the initial assumptions you've made in Exercises One through Ten.

When you contact an organization, find the person who has the job you want to test drive. Call and arrange an appointment to ask them about their organization and their job duties. This is not a job interview; this is an informational interview, a career research survey.

At the interview, as much as possible you want to see the work environment where this person spends their time. Shake hands and introduce yourself to others working nearby; try to get a flavor for the kinds of people with whom you might minister as teammates. Ask questions that relate to your passion and your talents. Get a feel for their corporate passion, to see if it matches your personal passion. Learn about their operations and methods to determine whether you'd be able to thrive by using your strengths in such an environment.

For cross-cultural ministry options, we recommend a short-term (say, two-week) trip to visit the person who has the job you are drawn to, in order to gain direct, preliminary exposure to the geographical setting and culture in which you're considering serving. Will you be working out of a pickup, in a modern building, in a cinderblock hut? Do you need to consider dietary issues, climate or other issues specific to the location? We Americans have it so good that, unless we have traveled to distant lands, we expect that one can always drink the tap water, have electricity 24/7 and shower every day. Your "field trip" will help you adjust your expectations to fit reality.

Visit your potential future work setting ahead of time.

When I (Nelson) visited Russia, I discovered that everything's broken, it's always cold, simple supplies like toilet paper are not available, and people don't make eye contact— they're so used to looking over their shoulders. The whole culture was like that, and it didn't take long to wear on me. Anyone can manage the frustration for a couple of weeks or months, then return home and talk about all the good parts. But then, if they decide to return for four years, they go in with accurate expectations and direction for mental preparation.

A study of 250 second-term missionaries revealed that they were considered successful because their past experience in their environment had prepared them mentally for future ministry. Their expectations were aligned with reality. No matter which service opportunity you are considering—stuffing envelopes in a church across town or preaching the gospel across the globe—

your ministry is more likely to succeed if you visit the work setting ahead of time. Even if the conditions are horrible, once you've had a chance to count the cost, you can focus more on the ministry fruit and the relationships you will build. That's part of the formula for success.

One missionary, arriving for a second term in Indonesia, said, "I'd recommend to anybody to go the second time first."

Just as We Were Told

The incarnation of God's Son was accompanied by great celebration. Glorious angels appeared to humble shepherds in the fields and told them about the newly arrived Messiah. The shepherds visited Jesus and His parents. And as they walked away, they marveled: "Everything was just as we were told."

In this book we've challenged you to take risks, to move forward, to take the next step. Frightening? Of course it is. But every believer in Jesus faces a daily question: Will you take God at His word? Will you choose to believe His promises? If you will, then one day you will realize...everything was just as you were told.

> *God is as good as His Word.*

God is as good as His word. He has given us a whole Bible full of truth about how life and ministry works best. He has revealed eternity and shown us clearly the true value of all things, temporal and eternal. He has provided prophecies and promises. And as we evaluate these truth claims, we continually confront the challenge: Either believe Him or don't. Can all of these "fantasies" and "fairy tales" really be true?

Whatever our choices now, at the end of life, when history's final earthly chapter has been written...all will turn out just as we've been told.

The rules of engagement in spiritual warfare? Just as we were told.

The value of our wood, hay and stubble, our gold, silver and precious stones? Just as we were told.

The eternal value and personal fulfillment from using our natural talents for God? Just as we were told.

It's all true! God's truth is bedrock firm.

Yet we struggle to believe it. We're distracted by the world's seemingly solid mirages. We're wealthy, and it's hard to sell out to ministry. We've been burned, and we're afraid to trust again. We're attached to the familiar, so anything different feels threatening. We've been conditioned to self-doubt; godly self-confidence seems unbelievable.

Believe it! Believe Him. Take seriously God's assignment for you. He has granted you responsibility to invest His resources for His kingdom. Whether you've got one breath left...or one hundred million...seek to spend them all in love for Him and for the people He places on your heart.

You *will* make a difference. Just as you were told.

Exercise Eleven
Validating Your Team and Task Selections

In order to experientially validate the selections you have made, it is important that you find someone who is doing the very job to which you aspire, within an organization that matches your passion. In completing the following steps, you should expect to visit organizations that have no job openings or that for other reasons you know you won't be working with. These contacts will be valuable in confirming your direction or helping you refine it.

1. In addition to exploring options in your own church, start collecting the names of ministry organizations of the types you've identified in Exercise Ten. A good place to start finding ministry organization names is the Ministry Web Directory at **ministrywebdirectory. com**. This unique web service is provided by Bible colleges and seminaries. They offer you their thousands of ministry contacts for your search. You'll also find listings for ministry vacancies and student internship options. Once on the website, select one school close to you and follow the instructions to complete a ministry search leading to a Primary Search Report. On this website you can use CONI numbers to identify specific organizations of any type.

    You can also find names of ministry organizations listed with the National Association of Evangelicals (**nae.net**) and the Evangelical Council for Financial Accountability (**ecfa.org**).

    If you are considering global missions, one of the best ways to get connected is to enter a personal service profile at **finishers.org**. There you will have the opportunity to build a marketplace/ministry resume. Some have said this free service is like a matching service, but for missions. You'll enjoy an interactive experience and receive a list of organizations that are surprisingly well suited to you and, if married, your spouse—matched to your interests, ranked by percent fit.

    As you research and find specific organizations you want to contact, write their names in the first column of the table below. Where possible, complete the second and third columns as well, but don't worry at this stage—you'll discover more contact names and information in Step 2 below.

Organization Name	Contact Person(s)	Contact Information

2. Once you've identified a few ministry organizations by name, inquire among friends and church leaders to see whether anyone knows a person who is part of those organizations—an "inside" person who might be a good point of contact. Let your friends help you complete the table above.

    Names of friends and church leaders I will ask for contacts within the organizations named above:

3. Call each organization's inside contact. Or if you cannot find an inside person for a given ministry, call and ask to talk with someone who is currently doing the job that you want to do. Describe the type of task you seek to perform. When you find someone at the organization who is performing that job, arrange to meet with them to observe and learn about the task. The following table might be helpful for tracking your appointments.

Organization	Contact Person	Meeting Place and Time

4. Go to the meeting at the organization's office, if it's within reasonable traveling distance. If the organization is not local, look for another similar organization that is local. You can later travel to distant, more promising locations for further research.

    When you meet with the person who is doing the job to which you aspire, ask questions about that person's ministry. Ask also about the organization, its leadership and the people with whom you'd work most closely. Just as important as knowing your job duties, you need to know your potential future team.

    On the next page we've provided a sample worksheet for notes from your informational interviews. You can make copies of this worksheet or adapt a format that works best for you.

Interview Notes

Organization: _____

Date: _____

Contact person: _____

The Team
What did you observe or learn about the organization?

Your response—Does the organization's passion resonate with yours? Is their ministry hitting the target (addressing the cause or need) that you want to hit? Do they provide a healthy, purpose-focused environment in which you would enjoy serving?

The Task
What did you observe or learn about the ministry job duties?

Your response—Is the task what you expected? Would you enjoy doing it? Does it make good use of your God-given talents at least 60 percent of the time?

Your Vision
What are your thoughts and impressions after praying about this opportunity?

Based on what you learned, do you need to revise your criteria for your ideal team or task? Explain.

Exercise Twelve
Your Ministry Job Search

At last! You're ready to begin searching in earnest for the unique, specific team and task God has prepared for you. Start following up on listings for available ministry jobs that appear to suit your passion and talents. Collect names of ministry organizations that turned up in your Internet and other research.

Now, you're welcome to follow the traditional job search path, filling out applications, sending off resumes. However, effective ministry job hunting does not rely solely on the resume. Resumes are helpful, but they will not get you a first appointment, nor are they likely to get you the ideal role for you. Other less-than-effective approaches are answering job vacancy ads and cold-calling blind with "I am looking for a job" e-mails. These techniques only work when your qualifications *exactly fit* the position you want to pursue.

So if the resume isn't the key, what is? It's the other R-word— "relationship." You need to connect through a relationship to gain the secret inside track for getting the perfect role. You need to know someone. Numerous surveys and studies into successful job hunting procedures show that 70 to 80 percent of positions are filled through a personal relationship, rather than by answering an ad. So consider a few suggestions for getting that important inside track—particularly for developing a relationship with the person who would be your future boss.

If you have the means to provide for your own financial needs, you might be happy volunteering your service without pay or raising support. Or perhaps a part-time income will cover your needs, and you can volunteer the remainder of your time in ministry. If you want to volunteer in order to establish relationships as a means to gaining a more responsible role or a paying position, it is better to refer to your service as an *internship* or *field experience*. These terms imply an understood goal beyond your current service. Once you've demonstrated your value to the ministry, and once you've gotten to know a number of the organization's staff, you are able to leapfrog one or more steps in the process we describe below. You might even be offered a position of greater responsibility or a paying job, without having to ask.

Keep in mind, you are offering to provide your service and in many cases to provide or raise the funds to do so. It is in these situations that life is most rewarding. The feedback Finishers Project has received from those who have made the conversion from a marketplace position to ministry is very often, "I am having the time of my life."

That said, how do you pursue a ministry job with an organization where you have no existing relationships? Following is our suggested procedure, by which you create a chain of new relationships linking you through your current acquaintances to your future boss:

1. **First link: People you know.** Begin by contacting your network of family, friends, pastors and church members. You're seeking names of people they know—in any position or department—inside the organization you want to pursue.

2. **Second link: Someone inside the organization.** Meet with that friend of a friend—your inside contact—in person (telephone and e-mail do not work as well). Explain your research and interest in the ministry organization. Express your interest in the position you are seeking and ask for the name and contact information of the department head or manager who could be your future boss.

3. **Third link: Your potential future boss.** You're going to pursue a series of two meetings with the manager or department head. Call to set up the first meeting. Mention the name of your inside contact: "I'm researching various ministries and their plans for growth. Karen Smith suggested that you might be a good person to help me." Ask for thirty minutes "to gather information regarding the future growth and new projects of your organization—particularly your program or department."

   Don't—repeat, *don't*—treat your first meeting as a job interview. No one on a first date asks, "Are you interested in marriage?" You're just beginning to cultivate this relationship.

4. **First meeting.** Do your homework before the meeting: Learn what the organization does and how they do it, so you can speak intelligently about the ministry's philosophy, programs, and departments. Start the meeting with "I would like to learn about growth initiatives in your department." Come prepared with a list of questions, and save some of them for your follow-up meeting. Asking perceptive questions demonstrates your awareness of and active interest in the organization.

Do not take your resume to this meeting or even suggest sending it. That would come across as a hidden agenda and would violate your stated purpose for the meeting.

If the manager or department head asks if you're looking for a service role or a job, answer something like this: "Should there be a position that fits my ministry goals, yes, I would like to discuss it. But my purpose is to get to know your perspective on the growth of your ministry." One of your questions might be "If the money were available, are there any new projects you would like to develop in the next year?" But in this meeting, it's premature to ask to be personally involved.

Afterward send a hand-written note thanking the person for his or her time.

5. **Second meeting.** About two weeks later, call and ask for a thirty-minute follow-up meeting. The topic of this meeting is further specifics about the department's future growth initiatives, hopefully including some new venture projects. Again, *do not* bring your resume to this meeting.

By this time you will have typically established enough of a relationship with the manager or department head to show interest in possibly working under him or her. The way to inquire about a possible ministry job is to wait until you have discovered a growth strategy or new project in the manager's plans. During the second meeting (or later), refer back to this growth strategy or new project, saying something like "I'm personally interested in the future growth projects you have planned. If at any point you think I might be able to help with them in some way, I'd appreciate the opportunity."

6. **Interview.** Once an opportunity is on the table, and you have previously met at least once with the department manager or recruitment director, now the resume becomes important. Be prepared to share how you can help the organization meet its goals. Explain your passion and your talents. If this pursuit is for a paying job, do not ask about salary, benefits, vacation, flex time, relocation expenses, or other particulars during the interviewing process. You can discuss this information after you receive an offer. Alternately, if the assignment is for a ministry position where you must provide or raise your own support, it is proper to ask for the terms of engagement.

7. **Research, negotiation, acceptance.** After you receive an offer but before you accept it, ask to meet with someone who works for the same director or manager. Inquire about this manger's style, especially how he or she gives guidance and correction. Have they had any difficulties with previous personnel?

If the position is for a paying job, only *after* you've received a job offer is it time to begin negotiating salary, benefits, and job duties. You're not likely to get everything you hope for, so negotiate with your minimum acceptable package in mind. Whether the job is paying, volunteer or support-based, significant among your concerns: Be sure that the team shares your passion and that the job makes good use of your natural talents at least 60 percent of the job's work hours.

You are not obligated to accept an offer until you're prayerfully satisfied that It's right. And your best move in some circumstances is to graciously decline, leaving the door open for future possibilities.

These search tips should open doors to many more positions than you'll find posted on an Internet source. It's all about relationships—who you know and who you take the time to get to know.

Remember that your first attempt at finding your ministry role does not need to be perfect, but it does need to reasonably reflect your personal passion and talents. Your informational interviews and your initial ministry job interviews will put wind in your sail. Learn from these and use them to make adjustments and corrections.

Here's a suggested checklist of preparatory resources and tasks that will facilitate your search and ensure greater success:

❏ Names of people you want to invite to your prayer and support team.
❏ Names of possible partners who may join with you in this pursuit.
❏ Your plan for prayer and listening for God's guidance.
❏ Your plan for prioritizing tasks and determining your next step.
❏ Various tasks, such as letters, e-mails, Facebook notes or thank you notes to write; practicing your presentation to ministry staff.
❏ Church pastoral staff you should communicate or meet with to discuss your plans.
❏ Research resources beyond those we've listed for you.
❏ Financial considerations.

❑ Transportation arrangements.
❑ An alternative plan—Plan B in case your Plan A takes an unexpected turn.

May God richly—and perhaps surprisingly—bless you as you follow your calling for this next season of your life.

Appendix A
From Nelson: Yes, God Can Use You!

I want to begin my story with the story of a couple who went before me—a couple who toiled with unnecessary frustration to grow, thrive and minister in hardpan soil that I've spent my latter decades working to soften for others.

Gene was at the end of a successful marketplace career as a vice president of a multinational corporation. He and his wife, Frances, were also heavily involved in their local church in leadership and mentoring roles, and in the church's missions program. They were also local area leaders and teachers in Bible Study Fellowship, a Bible teaching and discussion ministry.

Retirement from the marketplace had been on their horizon for several years; in reality it would be a transition from one career to another. Gene and Frances had been sensing a desire to explore some type of ministry service. But at fifty-nine they had no clear idea as to where they would fit. They would find their direction, but it would take them three long years.

Although they were not gifted at evangelism, they were passionate to make a difference for God. By trial and error, they discarded several ministry options. They considered counseling, for example—a cause that they knew was worthy of their energies, but not one that energized them personally. After more searching, the couple's persistence finally paid off, and they found a place for their gifting and experience in Africa, participating with a leading American sending organization. They had spent part of their life in Puerto Rico, where Gene had picked up some Spanish and a little Portuguese. So they knew they had a head start when the government of Mozambique, a Portuguese-speaking African country, invited Americans to provide a morals-based curriculum in their schools. They both spent several months in Portugal to enhance his grasp of the language.

By the time the couple reached Mozambique, they encountered roadblocks preventing them from fulfilling their original assignment. This often happens in ministry. But it pays to be flexible and, rather than giving up, Gene and Frances decided to stay and search for the reason God had brought them here. In the end they were placed, not in the schools, but in charge of launching an entire Bible study ministry, where they applied their familiarity with Bible study methods. Gene also drew upon his business expertise, using his experience with managing and organizing people to shape the new ministry. They went in with an end-game strategy to train up enough nationals to leave the ministry in their hands. Because of their investment, hundreds of believers in Mozambique, with a variety of gifts, have been empowered to impact far more lives than one couple ever could have touched by themselves.

How I Got into This Thing Called Finishers Project

I was about to turn fifty in 1996, working as a chemical engineer and director of research in a multi-national company, when I became aware of stories like that of Gene and Frances. I became troubled that *anyone*—of any age, with any talent and a wealth of experience—should have to hunt several years before finding a significant role in ministry. With the prospect of hundreds of thousands of Evangelical baby boomers exiting the turnstiles of the workplace every year, this situation just didn't seem right. I was prompted by the Lord to challenge my generation to love and good works and to make the rough places plain. I was moved to help simplify the process of connecting would-be workers with overseas ministry organizations.

I was born in 1946, on the leading edge of the baby boomer generation. The wave of boomers that had been surging relentlessly for decades up the timeline was approaching retirement age. An increasing number of people were beginning to inquire about ministry opportunities. But the ministry organizations didn't know what to do with them. In the mid-90s, if a mission organization received a phone inquiry from anyone over thirty-five, they did not know who to put the call through to.

Something has to be done, I thought to myself. So I offered ideas to mission agency leaders. But nothing happened. It was clear that I had to take initiative.

About that same time, I was reading in Matthew 9 and ran across the familiar verses 37–38, where Jesus said, "The harvest truly is plentiful, but the laborers are few. Therefore pray the Lord of the harvest to send out laborers into His harvest." It became clear to me that the only action verbs in this passage are "pray" (my responsibility) and "send" (God's responsibility). My response? I agreed to work prayerfully on the assignment He was putting on my heart and to trust the Lord that He would hold up His end of the bargain to send more laborers. I could not change the world. But God was prompting me to do something I *could* do. He was asking me to pray for something He already wanted to accomplish.

There are times in our lives when we feel so intense about something that we make eye contact with God. For me this was one of those times. As I prayed, God clarified my direction. His task for me was simply to clear a pathway—an avenue by which midcareer and older people could enter ministry service. Using my networking and project management skills, I began to attend the mission industry association meetings, making connections, sharing my dream. I knew I was no expert in the missions industry, but I determined before God to pursue this as far as it would go, until I hit a barrier. There was no barrier. Thus was born the Finishers Project. Slowly I established in others' eyes my credibility and competency to place people into ministry.

I was following my own calling. Three factors merged in this process. First, I understood my unique gifting—the way I am constructed to use entrepreneurial, networking and project skills. The same natural talents I had used in my career as a researcher carried over into my ministry experience. In both cases I lived with a high level of ambiguity. Second, I had a measure of faith, to trust the Lord to do a better job with my life and my agenda than I could. A simple faith that the Lord would accomplish what He already wanted to do. And third, I was intrinsically motivated. I didn't need someone else to pump me up or push me along. After spending years building a relationship with the Lord, I wanted my life to count. Besides, I find it energizing and motivating to exercise my gifts—sharing ideas and taking the lead to bring them to fruition. Ideas are a dime a dozen. I have a lot of these dimes. For me, taking action to bring the best and biggest ideas to reality is very motivating.

The most fulfilling fruit? In a little over a decade, Finishers Project has guided thousands of people to ministry organizations and successfully placed them locally and around the world.

My particular passion was to facilitate the match between a person seeking to serve and the ministry organizations seeking those willing to serve with them. Eventually my assignment changed. My strength is to start something, rather than run something. With Finishers Project well established, the organization has successfully transitioned to another leader, while I have taken the assignment to start other mission recruiting initiatives in the US and in other nations.

Along the way, I've learned surprising and simple principles about God's plan for using *anyone* in a well-matched ministry role *anywhere*. These apply just as well to a twenty-five-year-old as to a fifty-five-year-old. And they work the same, whether you are prompted to serve across an ocean or across the street. If you are willing to serve God and others, rather than only serving yourself, He has a place for you.

You Can Make a Global Impact

I believe that those of us who came of age in 1960s and early 70s were the children of the dream to change the world, without war. We were disillusioned by Vietnam and wanted to accomplish something different than our parents—the so-called GI Generation—had done. We understood: The higher the risk, the higher the reward. And we were pushing for change.

Then we became distracted raising kids, developing careers, paying off mortgages. Still, the leopard cannot change its spots, nor did our generation lose the dream. Deep inside we still long to make that difference. Our experience now seems parallel to that of Moses. He set out as a young man to change the world—a Hebrew trained in the ways of corporate Egypt, at the peak of his career and prowess. But it wasn't God's plan to use Moses in that condition. It wasn't until he was an old man—possessing life experience that Moses hadn't realized he needed—that God said, "Okay, now you're ready." Similarly, many of us are still looking forward to our greater works.

Let's think globally. Almost any place in the world, you can make a difference. It is easier than ever before. Americans possess an abundance of useful life skills that are desperately needed most anywhere. Many of us Westerners are prone to want to invest ourselves in non-Western contexts. We quickly come to appreciate that we are more highly and broadly skilled than we ever realized, and it's not difficult for us to make a difference anywhere in the world...*as long as we come to serve nationals.* I stress this last caveat, because we Westerners tend to be fixers, and the nationals don't want to be fixed. We must come with a servant's mindset, not to run the show. At most, where appropriate, we may be called to coach those nationals who aspire to leadership to lead in their own community or country.

The doors are wide open. English is the closest thing to a world language that has ever existed; virtually all nationalities are learning it. American TV is shown around the globe. Therefore we can go most anywhere and communicate, even with limited language training. We live in a wonderful day when the nations are open and receptive—not necessarily always to be evangelized, but open for business, for enterprise, for education, and even for help with government. When the Iron Curtain fell, Russia quickly began hinting: "Please, don't send us any more evangelists. We have plenty of those. Can you send us Christians that can actually *do* anything?" The nations of the world are begging us to come with our skills, talents, training...to train *them* how to do the real work—not to do the work ourselves. After all, on reflection, that's really what the Lord asked us to do in the first place—to disciple the nations. A disciple is literally a "learner." We are called to go as teachers and trainers.

At our Finishers Forum events we do a workshop titled "The Range of Opportunities in Missions." In that session, a panel of agency recruiters sits up front. Then audience participants provide a little of their life stories—training, occupations, volunteer activities, church background, family situation and so forth. The panel is then asked, How can a person like this be used in missions? Without fail, agency recruiters lay out numerous options for each individual, couple or family. I guarantee, the same would be the case if you were to articulate your story with organizations who are reaching the nations. In fact, you can do so now by completing a profile on the web at *finishers.org*. One woman filled out her profile, convinced that she was too ordinary, that her life was too pedestrian, and she would not be found useful. She was amazed to receive contacts from several organizations, offering her options that matched up with her criteria for serving. She was somewhere between surprised and grateful to discovered that she indeed played a significant role in the Great Commission.

We can use whatever occupational skills, life skills, communication skills and functional skills we have...to train people in the arena of our individual passions. We must take initiative, be proactive to get out there and boldly stride down any path. The Lord will make the way. The only alternative is that we'll miss out—that we'll retire to the comfort and safety of heaven, hoping that someone takes up the challenge we missed.

For the children of the 1960s and 70s, time has honed us. We've added experience and skills to our ideals—ideals we still hold dear. We've been prepared in ways that were not available to our parents. Earlier generations couldn't just board an airplane and travel to another land to serve God—and get there within a day. We can. Without thinking twice, we can visit anywhere in the world. All to be part of the end game—that is, to see the knowledge of the glory of the Lord fill our neighborhood, fill our nation and fill the earth, as the waters cover the sea. There is no limit with God. He is a big God.

The only limit is governed by our willingness to see Him as He is. How big is your God?

Appendix B
From John: How I Got into This Thing Called IDAK Group

You'll probably understand my career-related role best by means of a contrast: Nelson's passion has been to awaken ministry organizations to receive the new wave of experienced workers for the harvest. My passion, on the other hand, has been to equip the worker to select his or her best-suited harvest tools and harvest field.

I started in the field of aptitude assessment the same way most in my generation started their careers—by accident. As a returning Vietnam veteran in Fort Worth, Texas, I needed a job. Because of my previous post-college headhunting experience, a minority-owned employment agency hired me to recruit and train African Americans to fulfill affirmative action quotas for Fortune 500 companies.

After about two years, I began to sense a prompting from God to advance my job from a paycheck to a calling. In order to do that, I needed more counseling experience and freedom to experiment with assessment systems. Three years at the University of California at Davis as a career advisor gave me opportunity to study the field of career guidance. In those days there were no graduate study programs for career counseling, let alone Biblical career counseling. I chose to pursue seminary education to give me a stronger foundation in God's Word for my work. I found a campus that allowed me to pursue my personal goal and provided personal coaching via my mentor, Dr. Grant Howard.

Seminary was a wonderful time of study and development. I was fortunate to supplement my classroom instruction with many extended coaching sessions with Dr. Howard. His oft-repeated question was: "Where do you find that supposition in the Bible?" He held me accountable to stay true to the Word of God. After two years of mentoring, Dr. Howard and I began to experiment with a leadership development seminar. Thus we laid the foundations of applying natural talents to one's calling.

In 1980 several colleagues and I founded IDAK Group. I continued to pursue research and study, received financial grants, and facilitated three doctoral dissertations with three colleagues. Throughout all of this, a list of natural talents and their definitions evolved. In addition, and almost as important, a process for testing for those talents also emerged. Since then it has been my continued joy to help men and women find and follow their calling by discovering their God-given identity.

Nelson and I connected and began to collaborate because of our mutual interest in guiding men and women to their optimum places of service.

For more of my personal development story, see "The Right Team, the Right Task" in Chapter 1.

Ministry
Web
Directory

it's your calling,
find your ministry...

and connect.

search, connect, go »

Connecting you with
ministry organizations

www.ministrywebdirectory.com

I Want to Make a Difference *Now*
Your Bridge to Global Impact
by Don Parrott, president of Finishers Project

You want your life to count...to leave a legacy...to make a difference. For many of us that desire becomes an elusive dream, obscured by the urgency of life's demands.

The great strength of this book is the refreshing message that those "demands" are actually the building blocks of significance. To make a difference our lives need substance and experience.

The daily grind, the ups and downs, the successes and failures all work together to form the maturity and wisdom needed to make an eternal impact. Every chapter in this book is strengthened with real-life stories of people who are making a difference...now!

Read this book if you are in your 20s or 30s to embrace life's demands and build character.

Read this book if you are in your 40s, 50s or 60s to chart your next steps in making a global impact!

Find it now on ***www.amazon.com***.

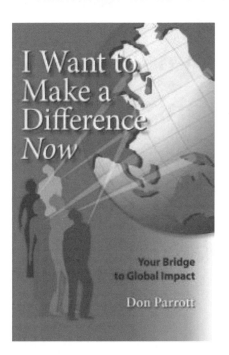

Don Parrott is a privileged husband, a proud father and a playful grandfather. He is a purposeful Christ-follower and a passionate leader. His life journey in raising a family of four, serving the church in North America and working cross-culturally overseas has uniquely prepared him for his current role as the president and CEO of The Finishers Project, an organization dedicated to connecting midlife adults with opportunities to make a difference with their lives.

TALENT DISCOVERY GUIDE

Everybody Has Natural Talents
- Discover what you naturally do best.
- Find how your talents can be matched to job positions.
- Develop a higher level of proficiency at your work.
- Identify your hidden talents.

Is This For You?
The Talent Discovery Guide is ideal for:
- College students
- Midcareer occupation change
- Employers
- Professionals
- Ministry professionals

Simple. Fast. Online Assessment
Want answers fast? Take the online assessment test and discover what your natural talents are. Simply complete the easy online test which will put results in your hands immediately. The optional validation process takes an additional 15 minutes.

Go to www.idakgroup.com/tdg